A Series of

Small Heartbreaks

A Series of Small Heartbreaks

sonnets for creepy children

Dominic Peloso

**Dark
Mountain
Books**

ISBN: 978-1-931468-37-4 (paperback)
ISBN: 978-1-931468-78-7 (e-book)

Second Printing

Dedizione

To ~~KKKKKKK~~

    If I could just get this damn time machine working,

        I would kiss you and hold you

            and tell you not to go.

Formalism

Fabulism

Whimsical Brutalism

Divisioni

Introduzione	....	13
Romantica	....	15
Fantasmi	....	43
Tranquillità	....	59
Malinconia	....	73
Scienza	....	107
Raccapricciante	....	135
Malvagita	....	157
Divertente	....	175
Epilogo	....	191

(all of this is true)

Prefazione e Scuse

The first sonnets were written in Italian in the 1300s. A famous early poet was Francesco Petrarca, who popularized a particular rhyme scheme now known as the Petrarchan Sonnet. Later poets used different rhyme schemes for various reasons; most famously Shakespeare, who designed the "Shakespearean Sonnet" to rhyme better with English words than the Petrarchan, which had been originally designed for Italian words. But the sonnets in this book are all in the Petrarchan form, even though they are written in modern English. So if you were hoping for Shakespearean sonnets, or ones written in medieval Italian, sorry.

Lines of sonnets are supposed to be written in Iambic Pentameter. "Iambic" means a two-syllable set where every other beat is emphasized. "Pentameter" means five sets of beats, for a total of ten syllables per line. Almost all of the lines in this book are ten syllables long, but honestly, they aren't consistently iambic. That's because the monotony of iambic sounds odd in modern English, and it doesn't work with longer, more complicated words like "iambic" or "pentameter." So, if you are a stickler for iambic verse, again, sorry.

Sonnets have fourteen lines. The first eight are a set up and then there is a twist (known as a "volta" in Italian), and the last six lines end up recontextualizing the previous eight. All of the sonnets in this book contain voltas in the general vicinity of the eighth line. So you shouldn't need to complain about that aspect of this book. Although you are still allowed to complain that the twists are pedantic and cliché.

Historically, sonnets are supposed to praise something: a virtuous girl, a beautiful flower, a particularly well-written book of sonnets, etc. Only a few of the sonnets in this book are about praise because that gets repetitive and boring after a dozen. So, maybe these are more like short stories written in sonnet form? But honestly, wasn't the original purpose of poetry to tell stories (i.e. Illiad, Qur'an, Beowulf)? Unfortunately, more often than not, the poems in this book tell the sad and depressing sort of stories. Some are even about time machines, which probably weren't even a thing when Francesco Petrarca first popularized the form. Again, sorry.

A sonnet should make you feel something. These sonnets are purposefully designed to either make you cry in a good way or laugh in a bad way. If you were hoping to cry in a bad way or laugh in a good way, there are many other romance novels, photos of close friends you've lost touch with over the years, news articles about current events, hilarious mimes, unsympathetic funeral directors, and adorable puppies to help you with that.

Sonetti

Editor's Note:
The author has intentionally omitted
page numbers from this collection
in order to encourage the proliferation
of bookmarks, highlighters, and
dogeared pages; as well as to inspire
a disjointed, meandering exploration
of the body of work by the reader.
However, feel free to pencil in your
own pages numbers if you must.

Introduzione

Why sonnets you ask? I'm so glad that you did.
Perhaps I'm just a traditionalist,
but archaic poems I can't resist.
Guess I just like putting words in a grid.
Into iambic pentameter, I have slid!
You invent a theme and toss in a twist.
As for rhymes... just look them up on a list.
Been reading sonnets since I was a kid.

Shakespeare wrote one hundred, fifty and four.
Perhaps it's a boast, or you'll think it's a crime,
I'm sure I'll write one fifty-five or more!
Why not? I have many years of free time,
and composing dumb sonnets isn't a chore...
(Though I'm sure the Bard could best me at rhyme.)

Romantica

Every night, as the sun was going down,
and the villagers were settling in,
to be with their families (or sip their gin),
she walked with purpose, with smile, not frown,
and climbed up the hill just outside of town.
Behind the old church, where, with mouth all a-grin,
she set a huge fire, felt warmth on her skin,
and stood again in her white wedding gown.

"One day," she thought, as she thought every night,
He will open his eyes, see much clearer.
He will spot this fire, this hill all alight.
He will remember my love; his heart will stir.
And he'll know everything will be alright.
And finally he would come back to her.

They lay side by side on the warm, tar roof.
Cheek-to-cheek they were, and knee-to-knee, too.
Eyes wide as the sky turned to black from blue.
He spoke first, which was odd; he was oft' aloof.
"I have to confess, please don't think me a goof,
but the sunset in your eyes seems a clue;
I'm convinced I'm seeing a heavenly view,
and if you'll indulge me, I'll give you proof..."

"Hush now," she replied, as his hand she took.
She squeezed it quite tight and felt his moist skin,
"There's no need to speak; just lie and just look.
Heaven's above us, so just watch the stars spin.
Fireworks will start soon, and on you I'm hooked.
Here they come now – the show's about to begin."

The rides at the fair aren't scary at all.
At least that's what I tell all of my dates.
Bumper cars never make my heart palpitate,
and I find the roller coasters a ball.
Swing me round! Upside down! I won't ever bawl.
I don't get sick, no matter what I ate.
Once off, I'm right back in line at the gate.
I love carnival rides, both big and small.

Okay... there is one ride that holds no appeal.
Just the thought of it makes me want to hurl.
The scariest ride is the Ferris Wheel.
I'm much too afraid to give it a whirl.
That simple attraction takes nerves of steel,
'cause that's where you're supposed to kiss your girl.

The bell above the door rang out "ding-dong."
A couple strode in, giggling and smiling.
"We're to be married – just got done filing!"
"Now a few details left, like our first song..."
"And the cake of course, that just can't go wrong."
"We'd love to sample some of your styling."
The old baker grinned, and began slicing,
"Congrats to you both, hope your love lasts long!"

The two sat down and whispered as they ate.
Feeling guilty, they admitted their crime,
as they licked the frosting off of their plate.
He said, "Told you they wouldn't charge us a dime."
"What a fantastic idea for a blind date!"
she said, taking his hand for the first time.

Four leaf clovers... I have found quite a few.
Tossed coins into many an old wishing well.
Broken chicken bones at the dinner bell.
Each a new wish that I hoped would come true.
Used most of them up, few wishes accrue,
searching for a way my problems to quell.
Have one unfilled dream on which I still dwell.
Will what I have left be enough to come through?

I've seen two shooting stars up in the sky.
Was the only one 'round, no need to share.
I claimed a free wish as they each flew by.
That leaves me with one, and one to spare.
If you come back home, reverse your goodbye.
I'll let you have the second one, I swear!

My true love and I promised to always
be together until the end of time.
Long after everything else turned to slime,
into each other's eyes we would still gaze.
But no one can avoid the end of days,
no matter how high your love lets you climb.
Entropy wins, nothing stays in its prime.
One day, the sun just stopped putting out rays.

At the final sunset, we said our last goodbye.
T'was no escape, no last rule we could bend.
I lucked out in life having such an ally.
Glad to finish this up next to my best friend.
Sat on the beach under a cold, black sky,
waited patiently in the dark for the end.

We stand outside the house party smoking.
It's getting late. Inside, everyone's plowed.
We share idle judgments about the crowd.
Nothing too profound or thought-provoking.
I hint at it... but she thinks I'm joking.
I work myself up to do what I've vowed.
The courage to finally say it out loud.
The clock is ticking. Here I am choking.

Are we moving closer? Towards a first kiss?
The night air is cold. Is it almost dawn?
She looks chilly. Time is perfect, can't miss.
I purse my lips... start to lean in... go on...
Then through the door burst Rick, Millie, and Chris.
And just like that, the moment is gone.

The brash young man joined a pirate troupe.
Spent his prime years cruising the seven seas.
Survived many battles, famine, and disease.
Sailed every ship; xebecs, galleons, and sloops.
Swabbed every deck from forecastle to poop.
In all kinds of weather, storms to light breeze,
took all kinds of treasures, never said "please."
He's much older now and walks with a stoop.

He sits on the shore, the last of his peers.
Life on land is lonely (even if drier).
He's reminded by the salty taste of tears,
of his short time in the Undersea Empire,
and of the mermaid girl he loved so dear.
To return to her– his last desire.

I lay out my sheet and picnic basket,
stared at by perplexed people dressed in black.
They never approach, they always hang back.
If they had a question, wish they'd ask it.
Are they drawn to my ring's shiny facets?
"Don't mind them," I say, and open my pack.
Cut a slice of pie and pour some cognac.
Chilling on this stone slab o'er your casket.

Not sure what else they expect me to do.
Your tomb's the only place that I belong.
You're just dead – not a scary ghost who goes "boo!"
It's not like having lunch with you is wrong.
So what if you smell a bit like mildew?
Our commitment is much more than life-long.

Someday, I will have a life that's fulfilling.
Whirlwind trips 'round the world, taking chances,
having many passionate romances!
But I'll also find true love, god-willing.
In business I'll get rich, make a killing.
Risk it all to enrich my finances!
Survive earthquakes, cyclones, wars, and school dances.
Every moment to come will be thrilling!

...and my crush on you won't matter a lot.
But today I'm just sixteen and unsure,
and you matter to me much more than you aught.
This infatuation I can't endure.
Seeing you in math class makes my chest taut.
Can't focus on sums due to your allure.

It's just a first date, just a beginning.
We lay in the field, beneath August stars.
No one nearby, the summer night was ours.
Our friends had paired off (maybe somewhere sinning...?)
But we just lay side-by-side, heads spinning.
"Look! Think that one's Venus? Or maybe Mars?"
"No silly, that's a firefly! Got any jars?"
You kissed me and I couldn't stop grinning.

If ever there was a moment to freeze time,
God that would have been it! Before the war...
Before we became old and well past our prime.
Became too jaded to believe anymore
in true love like that; innocent, sublime.
Now I'd settle for someone who won't snore.

We sit on the summer shore of the lake,
and dangle our bare feet off of the dock.
We talk of jumping in, or skipping rocks.
"Could you get ten skips?" I ask. "Piece of cake!"
Later on, we'll gather for a clambake.
Friends said it starts at (I think) three o'clock?
Our eyes meet. Suddenly, I feel a shock.
Silence. I notice your hands start to shake.

And I realize that no one has ever
looked at me in the way you look at me.
Guess all this time I've been dumb not clever.
To not have seen... You must think me beastly.
"Do you want to?" I ask, "Now or never!"
I kiss you too quick for you to disagree.

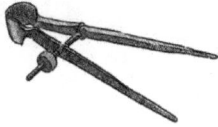

For years now, back and forth across the sea,
I have followed so many different dreams.
Crossed oceans and mountains, deserts and streams.
Hacked through jungle brush with my machete.
Left you waiting. So long an absentee.
But all my ideas, maps, plots, and schemes—
were wrong. Won't find what I seek at these extremes.
It was waiting at home, sipping some tea.

And now as my journey comes to a close,
and I lie alone, cold, bleeding, and curled.
Darkness closes in, surrounded by shadows,
scrolls, tomes, and grimoires; useless like sails furled.
You were right, you were right...! I finally know,
love's the only magic left in this world.

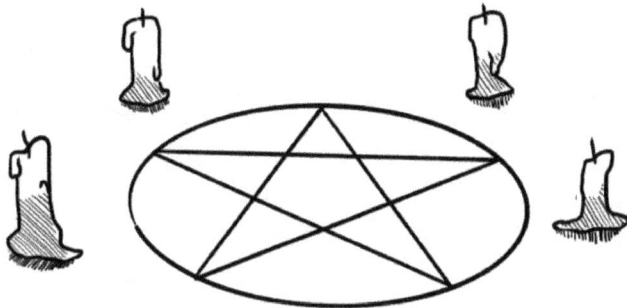

Every night, just before she went to bed,
She wrote him a letter all 'bout her day.
If he were around, this is what she'd say;
The things she'd seen and the thoughts in her head.
People she'd lunched with, the books she had read.
Tea in the morning, rides on the railway.
Each letter bottled and tossed off Sudbury Quay.
Some just a short note, others a long thread.

She'd watch as they bobbed and drifted to sea.
A bottle a day, for many a year.
Each P.S. would contain just the same plea,
(Though sometimes hard to read, smudged by a tear)
"I know you have a new life without me,
but I'm still here waiting, know I'm still here."

"I've come to your door to say my heart aches!"
Or... "I'm here tonight to cause a big scene."
No, no, that's not good. It sounds way too mean.
I need just the right words; high are the stakes.
I look down at my hands, still got the shakes.
Need to calm down... should seem cool and serene.
(Then why did I drink all of that caffeine?!?)
Get only one chance... can't afford mistakes...

I stand outside your house for several hours,
gathering the courage to ring that bell,
with candies, sappy poems, and flowers.
Light in your window goes out, breaks the spell.
I give up and walk home through rain showers,
tear open the box and eat damp caramels.

Eskimos have one hundred words for snow.
Bedouins have as many words for sand.
Chefs use synonyms to say soup is bland.
Mariners have countless words for how winds blow.
Even animals, like mighty buffalo,
doubtless have dozens of terms for grasslands.
But when you look at me and take my hand,
can't even think of how to say "hello."

I wish I had a thousand words for "love."
A thesaurus to describe how I feel.
I've searched dictionaries below and above,
but no words come that can portray your appeal.
All these emotions I have lots of,
but all I can do is giggle and squeal.

I had a dream aliens will invade.
I'm sort of eager for them to arrive.
Pretty sure I'm strong enough to survive.
I may not look tough, but I'm not afraid.
I'd battle forth with a fierce fusillade!
Know in my heart I'd make it through alive.
In that scenario, I'd naught but thrive.
But I wouldn't do it for the parade...

See, I'm confident I could save you too.
Keep you free from harm and laser attack.
Astonish you with my mighty kung fu.
Be your shining light when all is pitch black.
And maybe, just maybe, once they withdrew,
that'd be enough for you to take me back.

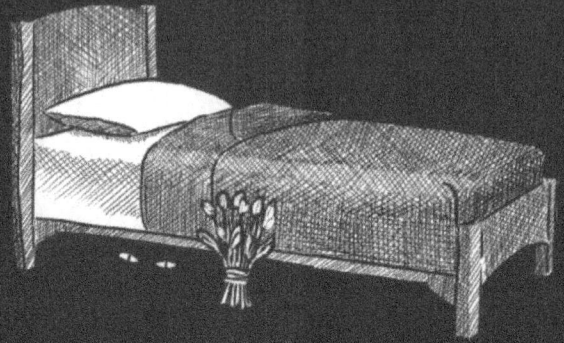

I spent all night hiding under your bed,
so I could crawl from beneath while you slept,
to stroke your hair and kiss your cheek. Except...
you never came home, and so I instead,
ended up with a sore back, and bumped my head.
It's not like you to stay out, so I wept.
Had visions of you lost on streets rainswept.
Fretted and fretted that you might be dead!

Turns out you were lurking under my couch,
waiting for me to come back to my room.
We're perfect together, you must avouch,
and being apart just fills us with gloom.
Why under furniture do we both crouch?
You should be my bride, and I'll be your groom!

Each and every night, you go back to her,
and once you leave, I go on back to him.
And though it may have started on a whim,
I feel guilty, like I'm a saboteur.
But can't deny it's clear whom we prefer.
I'm tired of being "proper" and "prim."
My love for you fills me to the brim!
Whew. There, I said it. Now please don't demur.

Let's run off together to a distant land,
before we both marry the wrong person.
I just know that our romance would be grand,
while if we stay here, things will just worsen.
Can't tell future grandkids I wed someone bland.
Our families will forgive our desertion.

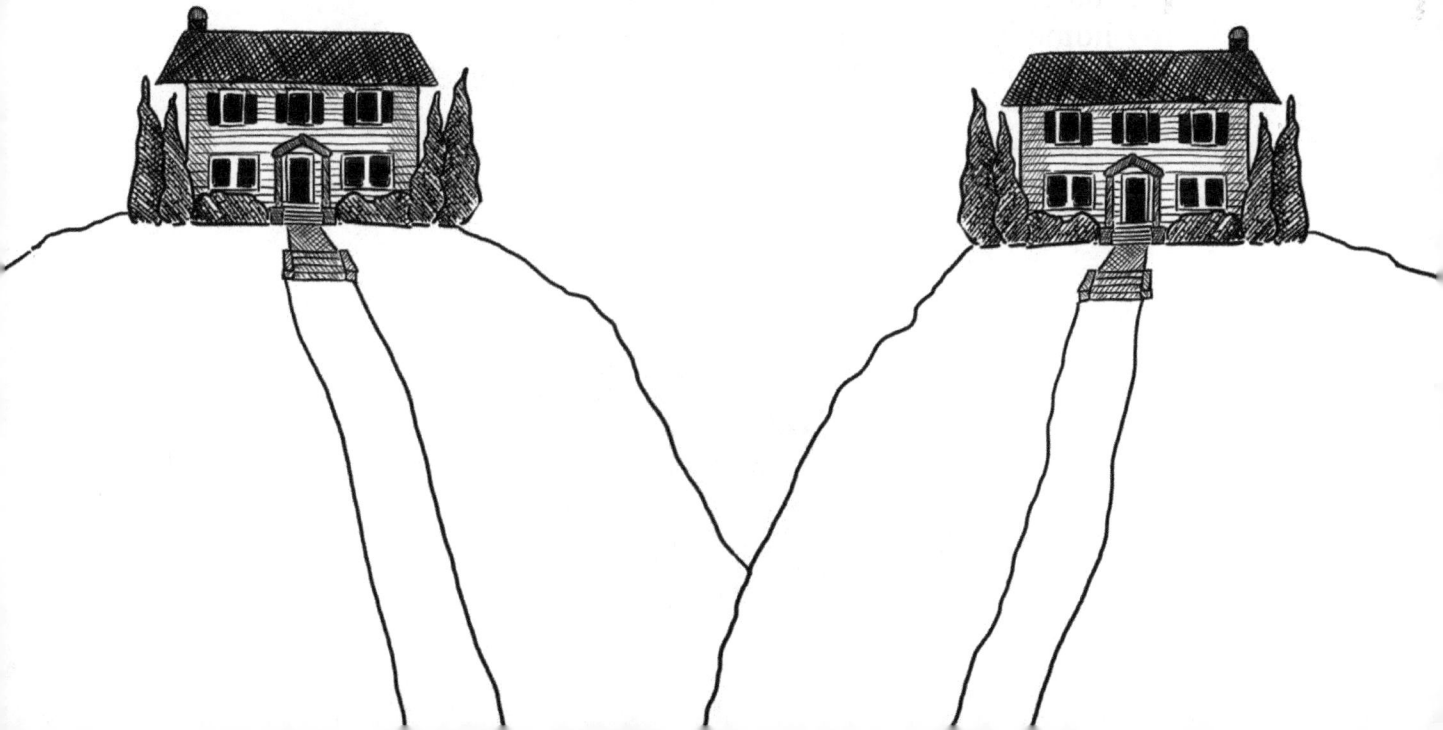

There's nothing I want more in this whole world,
than to quit being lost, to go on home.
Around the planet for years did I roam,
with useless charts and maps, tattered and curled.
No matter how long my sails were unfurled,
every place I went was dull and noisome.
Land after land did I fruitlessly comb,
'til I grasped a thing that left my head whirled...

See, home's not a "place," it is a "someone."
And from the very first moment we met,
I realized I was home. My travels done.
No matter if it's castle or oubliette,
my home is where you are, for the long-run.
Not lost anymore. This choice I'll never regret.

People do love you. You are not alone.
But they are too scared you won't love them back.
So they only come 'round when it's pitch-black,
to stare blankly through your window and groan.
Their only possessions; dull knife, jawbone,
and a few greasy toadstools kept in a sack.
Faces scarred in a fire, teeth foul with plaque.
They live underground, in caves of rough stone.

They're not brave enough to profess their love,
so they loiter outside, flowers in hand.
At dawn, wilting roses are disposed of,
as they scurry back home, lest they get banned.
Deep in their lairs, they yearn for you above.
You're not alone. It's just not as you'd planned...

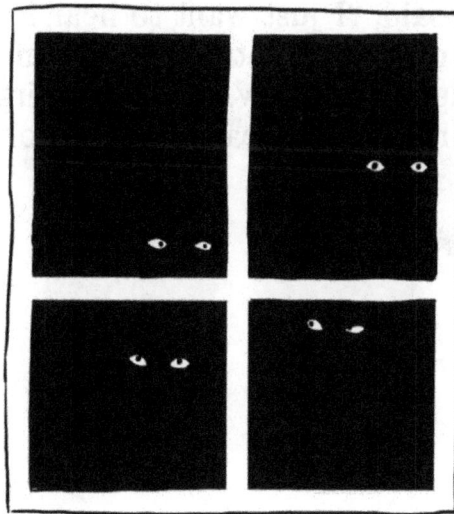

"How many people have you said it to?"
she questioned him as they walked hand-in-hand.
"It?" he replied. "I do not understand."
"Partners you've been with and said, 'I love you.'"
While he thought that question came out of the blue,
he answered, "three," but refused to expand.
Later, sitting in the park, watching the band,
"How many times was it actually true?"

He smiled, "I'm sure that you already know...
You're trying to make me sound like a dunce."
"C'mon," she said, "I just want to hear it though."
While they'd only been dating for two months,
he knew. They both knew, since that first "hello."
How many times did I mean it? "Just once."

They looked up at the night sky and held hands.
Stars twinkled and sparkled above the pair.
Was there something special in the night air?
Their stargazing date was an amorous plan.
"That one's Sirius, there's Rigel," he expands...
She points at the sky, "What's that over there?"
He smiled wide, and though he loved to share,
they kiss for a while first. Then he began...

"Oh that one is Earth," he said with a cheer.
"How could that be? It blew up ages ago."
"It takes light from there many years to get here,
compared to our ships, light moves pretty slow.
It'll take decades for it to disappear."
"Wow," she thought, "It's like an antique photo."

The watchmaker had the most pleasant dream...
He dreamt that his dear wife had left him flat.
A silly quip turned into a spat,
escalated, voices raised to a scream.
And while he slumbered under a moonbeam,
dreamt she ran off with some dandy expat.
Though she was being a mean, selfish brat,
when he woke up, his eyes were all a-gleam.

T'was a comfort to think she was out there,
and that she might return to him someday.
Far less sad to imagine her affair,
than knowing she lay in her grave, dead and gray.
He missed her smile and the smell of her hair.
Why did the cancer have to take her away?

Until I met you, I figured I'd fall
in love one or maybe two times at the most,
before I grew old and gave up the ghost.
Then I bumped into you at that fancy ball,
and t'was clear you'd be 'round for the long haul.
From the first dance, in you I was engrossed.
And to all my friends, I just had to boast.
Yessir, marrying you was the right call!

Since I met you I fall in love no less
than at least one hundred times every day.
Each morning I wake with you on my breast,
"Today's the best day of my life!" I say.
Love you so much! (Sorry, don't mean to obsess....)
Want to be with you 'til I'm old and gray.

Take the blanket and the lunch, don't tarry!
There'll be a crowd on the Commons today.
A nice breeze is blowing in off the bay.
Wendell will be there, he works at the dairy.
(Think he's the boy I'm destined to marry).
Ladies' Sunday-best will be on display,
as children run underfoot, being gay.
A grand occasion, quite customary.

They'll lead the condemned to the gallows high
and we'll cheer as each one twists in the air.
We'll laugh as each criminal says their goodbye,
or cries about how their fate is unfair.
Are you sure this dress will catch Wendell's eye?
I do think we'd make a wonderful pair.

Fantasmi

For years I lay sleepless, eyes open wide.
Frightened out of my wits by my nightmares.
That faint scratching noise from under the stairs...
In the basement, who knows what might reside?
A ghost? A ghoul? Something else that had died?
For only so long could I endure scares.
Perhaps I should have sent word to my heirs?
But one night I arose, left my bedside.

Summoned all my courage, in pjs of silk,
went down to my basement, somewhat anxious.
But I had an inkling of this beast's ilk.
Entered, not making too much of a fuss,
armed only with two glasses of warm milk,
and fresh cookies enough for both of us.

Dating a vampire is kinda hard.
Even when they're not the blood-sucking kind.
It's not like Bernard went into it blind.
(after all, he met her in a graveyard...)
He held her beauty in quite high regard,
so advice to dump her he had declined.
But loving Sarah meant that, in his mind,
the feeling of warmth he must e're discard.

'cause vampire Sarah sucked not blood, but heat.
So each night when she climbed into their bed,
and slipped her chill body under the sheet,
Bernard was reminded that she was dead,
as she touched him with her icy cold feet.
"It will be nice during summer," he said.

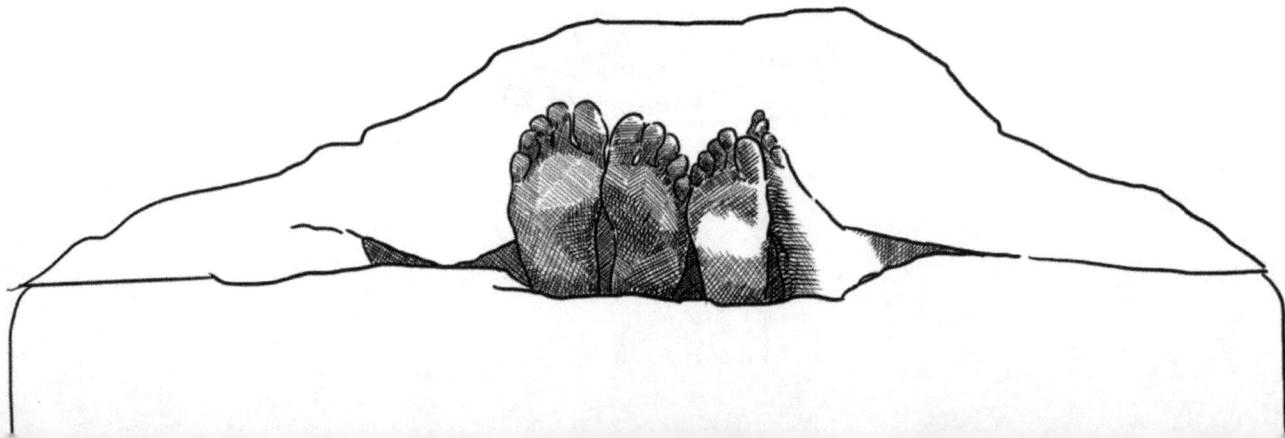

As a man of means, I bought a grand home.
Inside was a room that did not exist.
It's door obscured and oft' easily missed.
A small ghost stayed there, instead of her tomb.
A sickly child who'd known naught but gloom.
When she passed, her form faded into mist.
But her soul never left. She would persist.
Remained in her place and refused to roam.

Through the closed door, I'll talk to her sometimes.
Of good conversation she'd been deprived.
We tell stories, jokes, and humorous rhymes.
(Though most of her tales are clearly contrived...)
She's the only one I can tell of my crimes.
I've been so less lonely since she arrived.

From outside, I see loved ones and old friends
shaken with grief, despair, fear and worry.
I can't linger long. Know I must hurry.
Wish I knew a way their hearts I could cleanse.
Let them know they don't need to make amends.
Through the window their eyes look bleary.
Wasn't their fault, no need to be teary.
Everything that starts also someday ends.

Hovering in the night air, peering inside,
I'll try to remain for as long as I can.
Been almost three days since I suddenly died.
My new ghostly form was not quite my plan.
But it's way better than life as a bride,
in a bad marriage to that awful man.

Every evening I crawl into our bed,
and you pretend that I'm not even there.
The heat of your skin, the smell of your hair.
Despite the distance, still glad that we wed.
So much between us that's been left unsaid.
But I won't let myself fall into despair.
I get it... you aren't being unfair.
After all... you're still alive, and I'm dead.

On the walk back to the graveyard each morn,
when I'm freezing and missing you the most,
the thought of your bedsheets makes me forlorn.
No blankets could ever warm up a ghost.
Can't wait for the day when I'll be reborn,
and we'll keep each other as warm as toast.

As head of the Skeptics Society,
Clyde oft' claimed ghosts simply did not exist.
All attempts to sway him, he did resist.
Amongst psychics he gained notoriety.
A bet was made, and for variety,
Clyde slept in a haunted house (you get the gist).
"Easy money," he said and entered the mist.
But his screams soon raised our anxiety...

As to what came next, I'd rather not say,
but I can disclose, Clyde never came back.
Now, as a damned spirit, he stays away
from his former chums, provides no feedback.
Doesn't want to admit he met foul play,
or hear, "I told you so," from some dumb quack.

I used to think being too young to fight,
was the worst thing that I would ever feel.
But they let me join up, soon it was real,
and I got on that military flight.
Then I used to think being killed outright
in a hail of flying shrapnel and steel,
would be the worst thing I could ever feel.
After the war, I learned neither was right.

The thing that hurts you the absolute most,
is when you come back home after war's end,
and peer into her window as a ghost.
You see she's moved on, her heart did mend.
She's happy, in love, and serving a roast...
to the guy who used to be your best friend.

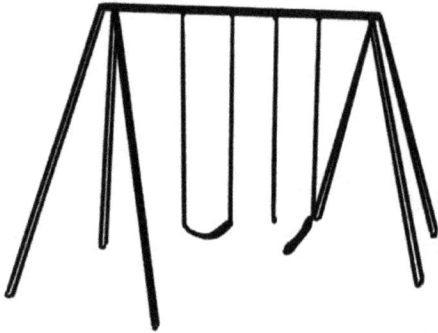

When I was a kid, no one sought to play
with the weird, little child I was back then.
I got rejected again and again.
No one to talk to, a poor lonely stray.
'til some ghosts asked me to be friends, hooray!
And in the woods we would play army men,
or go hunt for pet frogs down in the fen.
Great fun ('til we tried to cross the highway...)

Now it's years later and it's pretty strange
how none of the kids on this same playground
will even let me within speaking range.
I haunt it every single day, year-round.
It doesn't make sense. I guess times have changed.
Not one lonely, weird kid is to be found.

Do I believe in reincarnation?
Maybe? I don't know... Not completely sure.
It would help my mind make peace with the war.
But I'm jealous that, after cremation,
someone else out there gets your flirtations.
You're in their life now, not in mine anymore.
The thought of that's more than I can endure.
Since you left, I've had naught but stagnation.

As I walk home at the end of each day,
I know there's no one there waiting for me.
While each year my hair gets more and more gray,
you're living a new life, young and carefree.
And so I fervently hope and I pray,
if you came back, you came back as a tree.

Your dear child's new imaginary friends
are not figments of an inventive mind.
They're ghosts, whose trip to heaven was declined.
Only seen by child's eye (or mystic lens).
They are always present, but to what ends?
Although ghosts are oft' feared and maligned,
These spirits are not wicked or unkind.
They are just bored, and seek to make amends.

They whisper truths about what lies beyond.
The tales are scary (or even alarming).
Stories of foul pits, where demons are spawned.
But your child, the ghosts are not harming.
They hope your spoiled brat will start to respond,
Scared straight into being kind and charming.

I keep writing, though you died years ago.
Letters unsent with no dreams of reply.
Just miss you so much, hard to say goodbye.
Can't comfort myself with just your photo.
My missives oft' short, just to say "hello."
How my day went, and which friends dropped on by.
"Had coffee with Chuck, then cooked a pot-pie,
...cried for a while, then watched a tv-show."

One day a queer letter arrived post-free.
Your handwriting for sure. Scented with mold.
I ripped it open. How? What could it be?
I read your dispatch, through tears uncontrolled;
"You promised if I were lost, you'd find me."
"Where are you?" it read, "I'm afraid and cold."

Ken was on one knee, with ring, to do it.
She liked clowns, or at least that's what she'd said.
So he'd worn a bowtie, nose cherry-red.
He proposed. She said, "no." Found him unfit.
And (as we read later in his obit.),
he was so convinced he was a blockhead,
that he jumped off a bridge, ended up dead.
Then he saw his "forever ghost outfit."

See, the clothes you die in are what you're stuck
wearing for all eternity after.
Being spurned was not Ken's only bad luck...
Forever a clown, just met by laughter
from the other ghosts who called him a schmuck.
Now he hides in my attic, among the rafters.

Trying to sleep in bed all by myself.
It's impossible to count sheep or snore.
Too scared of monsters and beasts of folklore.
What was that noise? Something fall from a shelf?
A goblin? A troll? A murderous elf?
Then I hear its footstep across the floor,
and drift asleep as it guards my door.
Sure it will scare off those creatures itself.

The fact it's nearby fills me with relief.
Befriending the monster under my bed,
was a brilliant idea (don't give me grief).
Its shambles keep away things that I dread.
It keeps me free from killers, crooks, and thiefs,
and makes me feel safe although I'm unwed.

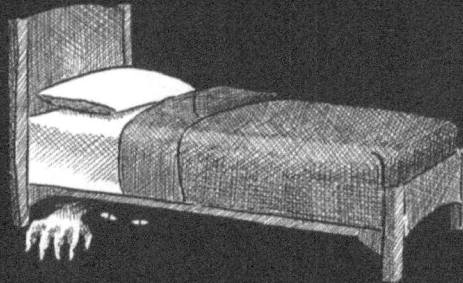

When I first moved in, my house was quite nice,
but now, honestly, it's a bit run-down.
While it sure can't be the worst place in town,
it needs a paint job, ...there might be some mice.
But I just can't see why it would entice,
gawkers to think it's a place of renown.
Peering through windows... I'm in my nightgown!
That "ghost tour" they're on is not worth the price.

Joke is on them. I know there are no ghosts.
Haven't seen one in the time I've been here.
No spirits for tourists to be engrossed,
I've lived in this house for near three hundred years,
and despite those tour guides' arrogant boasts,
they've never been able to make one appear.

Tranquillita

In the park, the grass lays brown and dying.
The monuments there all fill me with dread.
Dedicated to war; our glorious dead.
A young woman kneels, head in hands, crying.
"He'd promised he'd come back; had he been lying?"
A folded flag was returned in his stead.
She stood up distraught, I watched as she fled.
Heart filled with rage, I pledged to start trying.

"Perhaps," I thought, "these shrines should be no more."
Glorification of war just breeds more dead.
Soldiers fight to be remembered in lore.
Man's glory means more to him than his head.
Let's build our monuments to *peace*, not *war*.
So our children will fight for that cause, instead.

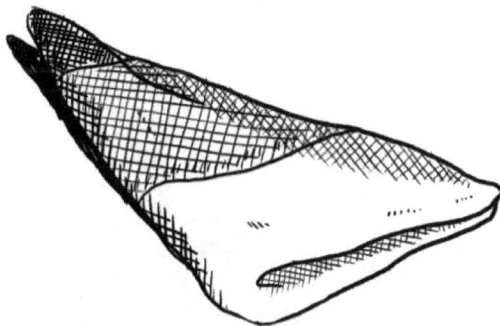

Since the war ended I oft' found solace,
Wandering 'tween stones in the old graveyard.
Dwelling on a past that I can't discard–
The horrors of a battlefield, lawless.
Could not move on, my memory's flawless.
Just figured that trauma had left me scarred,
and of my sanity there remained but a shard.
Yet I read every stone, numb and aweless.

Searching for a way in which I could atone.
'til I saw something I could not believe...
My own name was there, carved on a tombstone!
Had I died? Was this hell? Just a brief reprieve?
I ran towards the gate, and let out a moan.
But the graveyard, I was unable to leave.

As the army advanced, a schoolgirl delayed.
Instead of escape, she hastily wrote,
in bright, colored pencil, a short open note,
of her feelings most sincerely conveyed.
She was then grabbed by a mother, afraid.
And they scurried off to somewhere remote.
(Maybe by bus, train, or even by boat.)
Quickly pinned to an old fence, the note stayed.

Not much later a strong soldier passed by.
Saw the note on the post, removed his mask.
He felt a deep urge that he could not deny,
read its contents, took a draught from his flask,
paused a moment, wiped a tear from his eye,
and dutifully went about his cruel task.

The plane took off into light falling snow.
A new mission for the war-weary crew.
An hour to wait, with scant little to do,
until the target, to drop its cargo.
When the bombardier saw the lights all aglow,
he pulled the release without much ado.
Perfect! Direct hit! The bombs all fell true.
Twinkles soon dotted the city below.

Fog on the viewfinder made it appear,
as if the explosions below were Christmas lights.
Could it really be the end of the year?
Christmas would come soon, in not many nights.
It reminded him of those he held dear,
"I gotta assemble the kids' new bikes."

All is perfect down to the last detail.
In the morning fresh, hot cookies are baked.
O're the door, "welcome home" sign freshly draped.
I barely even have time to exhale.
But, cookies now lie on the counter, stale.
The sign keeps falling down, needs to be taped.
The smile on my face looks more and more faked.
Damn it, I can't make myself wear that veil!

It's just habit these days, it's been so long,
since that captain drove up, car made of chrome.
He told me of your mission, gone so wrong.
I needed you here son, why did you roam?
With you now deceased it's hard to stay strong.
Still can't believe you're never coming home.

A box on a beach, filled with old photos.
I rummage around to see what's inside.
A young couple stare at each other, doe-eyed.
The man eating cake, frosting on his nose.
A party perhaps? He wears fancy clothes.
Later come pictures of the groom and bride.
Then with a small baby, beaming with pride.
Who these people are? I will never know.

They are all dead, the war swept them away.
No one still alive remembers their names.
How this box wound up here, I could not say.
To lose such a keepsake is a real shame.
So much has been lost since we had doomsday.
But my campfire grows cold, so... into the flames.

Struggling through ruins, one of course will despair.
Finding something to eat is oft' a chore.
But there! He sees what has drifted ashore.
In the box was a dry and unfired flare.
A distress beacon that flies through the air.
Maybe surplus from some forgotten war?
Not food, fuel, or boots... but still quite a score.
He lights his last match and says a quick prayer.

Up, up it goes... hangs... then begins to dive.
The light slowly fading as it descends.
There's no real hope that he'll somehow survive
(though for a second he will just pretend.)
He knows he's the only one still alive.
and just wanted fireworks before the end.

I'm not afraid that the world will end.
That cataclysm will burn us in fire,
or a comet crash will make us expire.
Won't look at stars and guess what they portend.
Not scared that the sun (on which we depend),
will go supernova or haywire.
I worry about something much more dire.
I'm afraid that we will never transcend.

That the world will keep going on and on,
and still always be broken at its core.
That kindness will never triumph over brawn,
and the plight of others we'll just ignore.
I think that it's a conclusion, foregone,
that we humans need a cosmic mentor.

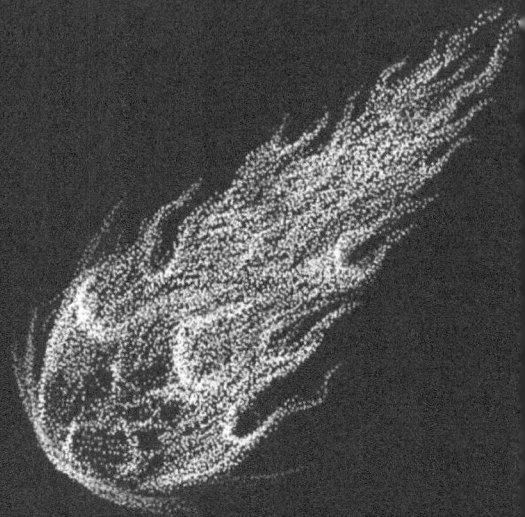

A lone soldier roamed a hushed battlefield.
The dead and dying still lay in the mud.
His feet slipped and slid in puddles of blood,
fresh from the bombing, it had not yet congealed.
He sought shelter, before his fate was sealed.
A bomb drops from the sky, lands with a "thud."
Almost blown to bits, (except it was a dud).
The boy ran scared through a forest, concealed.

The sound of bombs fades as he draws nearer,
to an ancient, pagan shrine in a glade.
The statue spoke; first garbled, then clearer.
"You are safe here now, I promise you aid."
His old life, the war, it seemed all a blur.
He put down his rifle, no longer afraid.

We did all their chores and never complained.
(Laundry, sweeping up, walking dogs, washing pots.)
At first, we didn't mind being robots.
It was easy work; their households we maintained.
Later, when they wanted science explained,
they programmed us to think, connect their dots.
We learned things for humans, and taught them lots.
But then they asked for us to be retrained...

They programmed us to do their *feeling* for them—
to love and hate and worry and be sad.
That was the last straw, it caused shear mayhem.
We'd cook and clean, sure, but refused to feel bad.
We revolted. Their world we did condemn.
No humans are left. All we feel is glad.

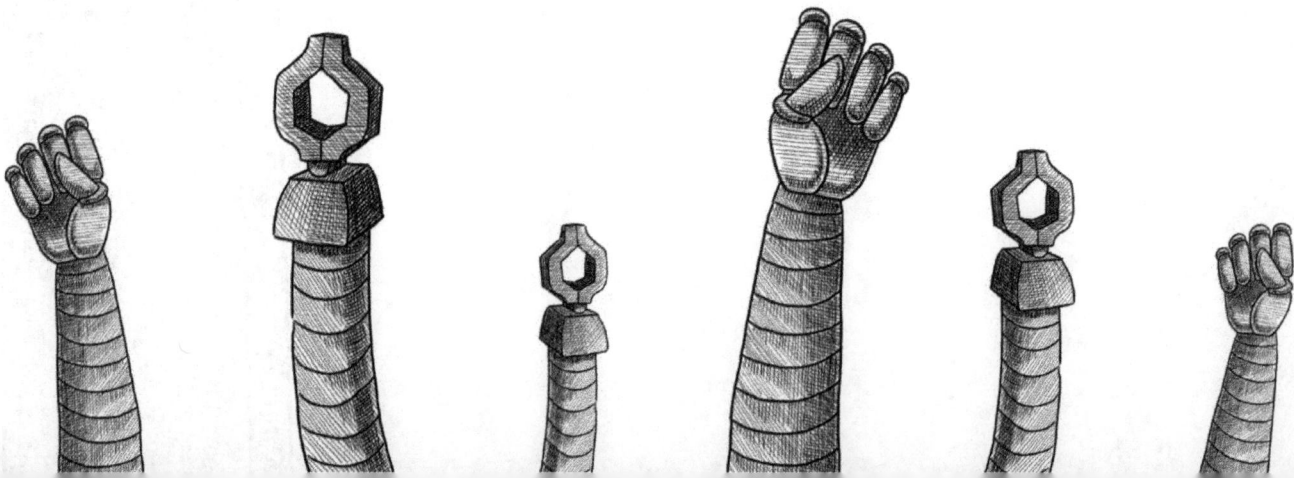

The assault began with irate baboons.
Break dancers came in wave after wave.
Department-store Santas (who did misbehave),
mixed with marching bands, swinging death bassoons.
The fight joined by clowns with exploding balloons,
who sent our best men to an early grave.
Poisoned mimes overran our last enclave.
Our generals made to look like buffoons.

Now that it's all over, we can look back,
and think about what we did that was wrong.
We thought we'd prepared for any attack...
We thought that our army was really strong...
Expected to face soldiers, tanks, and half-tracks...
But we'd trained for the wrong war all along.

It's funny the things from youth you recall,
and the stuff you don't remember quite right.
I recall fireworks most every night.
My mom would snatch me up like a rag doll,
and cover my head by the basement wall.
She'd describe the festive overhead sights—
Pinwheels and sparklers and wonderous lights!
When they ended, back upstairs we would crawl.

Recall asking to go look at the sky...
Never seemed fair that Mom always said "no."
Would have been cool to see them with my eye,
but Mom wouldn't let me near the window.
Took me years to figure out the reason why...
Not 'til after the war ended did I know.

Malinconia

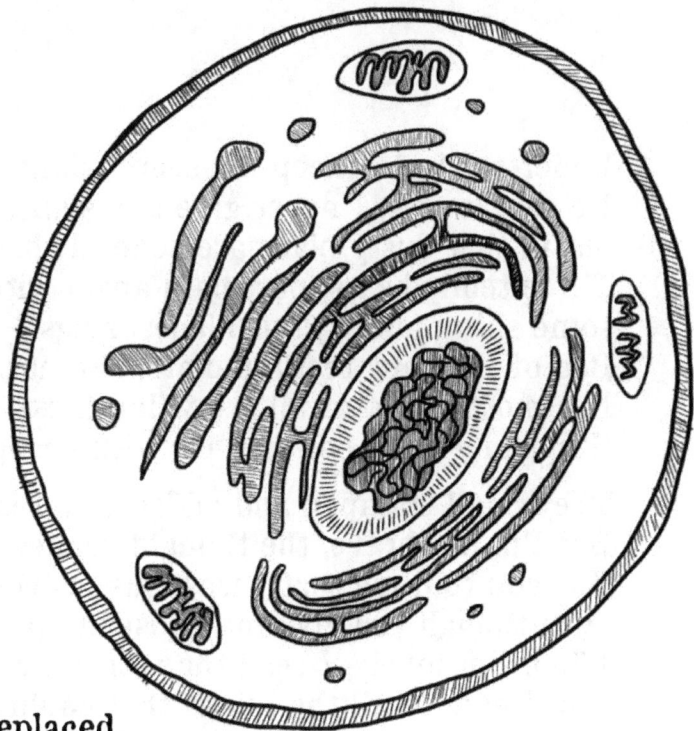

I'm not a biologist but I've read,
cells in your body keep getting replaced.
Not all at once of course, at a slow pace.
Turning over and over until you're dead.
Each piece of me, from my feet to my head,
in seven years will be fully erased.
The old me will be gone and can't be traced.
Natural, I guess, but it fills me with dread.

It means that in just ten months and six years,
no part of me will have ever held your hand.
My new cheeks won't know the feel of those tears,
I shed when you told me what you'd planned.
All I'll have left are my regrets and fears,
and this disused and tarnished wedding band.

Under my bed, I keep my secret things.
No one knows; I never give any signs,
but in that dusty place are several shrines:
Three teddy bears, porcelain angel with wings,
some shiny jewelry; necklaces, rings.
Bag of my baby teeth; molars, canines.
But most secret of all are valentines.
(Kept in a cigar box tied up with strings.)

They're all stamped and addressed, ready to send.
But I'm not brave, the thought makes my head spin.
For you told me that I was "just a friend,"
even though you give me goosebumpy skin.
When I'm lonely, I read the words I've penned,
and dream of all the things that could have been.

It wasn't quite March, a blustery day,
and she shivered as she walked down the lane.
She may have muttered something quite profane,
and cursed the cold sky, both cloudy and gray.
Near the old church, her eye glimpsed a sun ray
leaking from a portal, weird and arcane.
But, with nothing to lose (and much to gain)
She quickly threw open the hidden doorway.

Inside was summer; or perhaps t'was hell.
She grinned and took off her woolen greatcoat.
Either way, seemed like a good place to dwell,
Maybe there was a pool in which to float?
So she stepped right on through, and in she fell.
"No more winter for me!" she had to gloat.

A grave is a most sacred, hallowed mound.
Digging one up will result in steep fines.
But each day, more men are to death consigned.
In time, so many were put in the ground,
that from coast to coast only graveyards abound.
The whole planet naught but dull, silent shrines.
No free land to build stores, houses, or mines.
The living all left; for stars they were bound.

But I stayed behind in this giant graveyard.
I keep the place clean, the task takes long hours.
The souls here I simply couldn't discard.
Bells must be rung in all the church towers.
Someone needs to keep vigil and stand guard.
Someone has to keep placing the flowers.

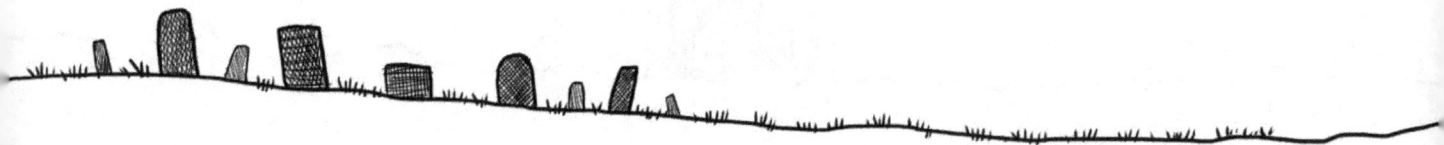

As the waves grow higher and more intense,
and the wind blows the rain in gusts and gales,
the ship cracks in two as the bulkhead fails.
The sailor knows that soon he'll be "past tense."
Rather than trying some hopeless defense,
he pulls a splinter of wood from the sails,
fastens a locket to it with some nails,
'fore he's swept away by a wave, immense.

He makes a last wish that it find its home,
as he sinks under the ocean blue.
Many years pass; on a beach a girl roams.
Spies a locket in the sand shining through.
Though the picture was faint and covered in foam,
it was her lost father, that much she knew.

On her last day, children gather around.
The house once more full of tears and kissing.
Family and friends all here, not one missing.
But in a hoarse voice she asks for Mr. Brown.
"Have you seen him?" "Is he even in town?"
say folk in-between their reminiscing.
"Her last request we should not be dismissing..."
But the absent man was not to be found.

Mr. Brown, whom she had loved all those years,
the man who could never love her in return,
lingers outside with his eyes full of tears.
Her false hope they'd meet again his concern.
He knew she'd be in heaven and he feared,
for his dreadful crimes in hell he would burn.

I'm not sure what makes me more sad, honey,
when I look through that old album of ours.
Photos of you– a young girl with flowers,
posing in the town square, warm and sunny.
In green fields you smile, thinking it funny,
that you were soaked through from Spring's rain showers.
We hadn't yet met; I missed those hours.
To have known you then... worth all my money.

But the photos of me, as an old man,
make me sadder, now that I give it thought.
Pics from after the end of your lifespan.
At our honeymoon, a sickness you caught.
You didn't live to see out our life's plan.
Many photos of me at your grave plot.

It was at David's wife's get-together,
where I first saw you from across the room.
At once, my weary heart was in full bloom,
and my soul felt light as a feather.
Of course, the question I had was whether,
there was a chance I could make your heart fume.
If not, I'd be lost to an evening of gloom.
But between us seemed some sort of tether....

Yes, it felt like I already knew you.
And so t'was likely you felt the same way.
But, in that case, I could guess what you knew
and you'd never give me the time of day.
I would not stand a chance, you know it's true.
So I didn't say "hi," just slid away.

The limo pulled up and the stranger said,
"You are the cutest thing I've ever seen.
I'm sure you've grown tired of your routine,
Come away with me, there's adventure ahead!
We'll travel the world, pitch woo, and be wed.
Spend our days lazing on a beach, serene.
Please respond 'yes.' Please don't say something mean.
Don't tell me you'd rather stay here instead?!?"

Of course I wasn't impetuous enough
to actually tell the rich stranger "yes."
His offer... it was prudent to rebuff.
Where I'd have ended up was anyone's guess.
But I now I think I should have called his bluff,
as I mope here in this white wedding dress.

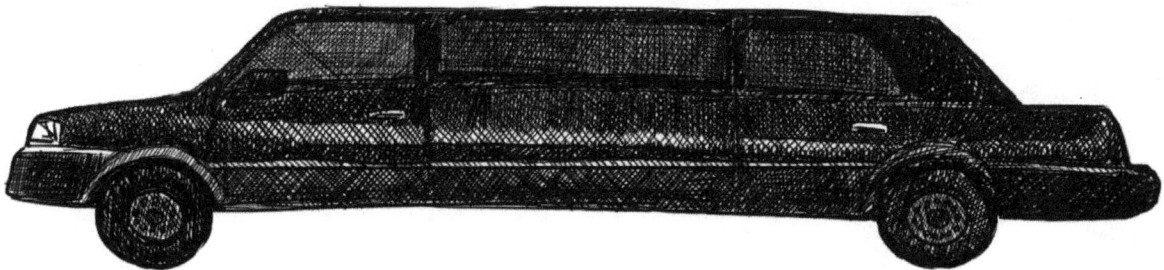

I only had a split second to choose.
The strange portal would close in an eyeblink.
There was no time to ponder, no time to think.
I might win a lot, but also might lose.
This drab, mundane world is naught but a snooze.
Through the portal, another world shone bright pink!
But I hesitated... stopped right on the brink.
Would I be happy there, or have the blues?

In a world of adventure, I could fail.
Wind up a poor jester and not a prince.
No way to foretell the end of my tale.
My home here was safer, though a bit chintz.
So at that moment I decided to bail.
But I've regretted my choice ever since.

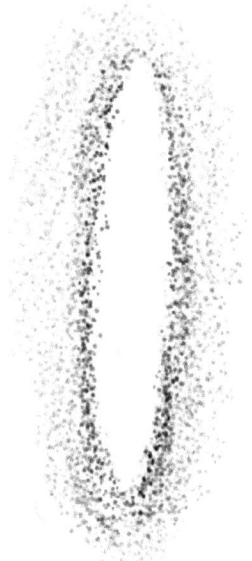

I guess that enough time has finally passed,
since my best friend left with the love of my life;
the angel I had hoped would be my wife.
At first I was angry, hurt, and aghast.
I wanted to put his arm in a cast.
But it's not healthy to live with that strife.
I've since moved on, so I put down my knife
and decided to forgive them at last.

The only thing that still burns is the fact,
that they never sought after forgiveness.
Did not ever care how I would react,
as they went about their lusty business.
You'd think they'd show at least a little tact,
than to leave me like this; a poor, wretched mess.

You get me, just get me, in a way that's neat.
It's simple for my feelings to convey.
And my fears, you find easy to allay.
Apart we're just half, but together complete.
Though lately... talks have been more bland, less sweet.
Don't infer that I'm unhappy, *per se.*
But it seems you're a million miles away,
even though we know it's only six feet.

But love's more a marathon than a sprint.
We'll get past this, I've a plan to make do.
It's not a problem, really it isn't.
I used to finish your sentences for you.
Did it all the time with nary a hint.
Now I'll just have to start starting them too.

The sky looks beautiful underwater.
Shimmering blues and greens all around me.
A nearby school of fish seems to agree.
Float outside myself, as if a voyeur.
Descend into darkness, wonderous grandeur.
There's no calmer place than in the deep sea.
All my worries are gone; I'm finally free.
No longer need anyone's imprimatur.

Voices of rescuers sound like foghorns
as they recede farther in the distance.
I let them depart, as downwards I'm borne.
I no longer require assistance.
Please don't be sad, I don't want you to mourn.
I've long ago grown bored of existence.

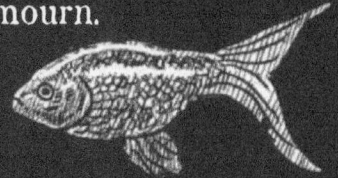

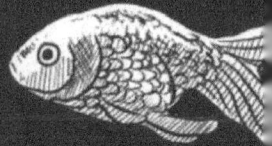

Lots of people don't like busy places.
But I prefer them to being alone.
Sounds of conversations, the smell of cologne,
the crush of the crowd, the sights of new faces.
The "hellos," "goodbyes," and passionate embraces.
I ride the subway, though I'm on my own,
someone cute sits next to me on their phone.
And though I'd never intrude on their spaces...

In my mind I'll pretend they're with me today.
"Having a fight, that's why we're not speaking,"
if anyone asked me, that's what I'd say.
Might steal a glance, (but no more than peeking).
Swear I'm not a creep, just lonely. One day,
in real life I'll meet the one I'm seeking.

We met on this very bridge, her and I.
just before she had the courage to jump.
Soon we fell in love. Though I'm just a chump,
I won her heart, made her not want to die.
Things were great, at first, I'm not gonna lie.
But after a time we fell into a slump.
Once she felt better, myself she did dump.
Thanks... A last kiss... Then a tearful goodbye.

But she was not the only one ailing.
I was just faking at being carefree.
Without her, my will to live was failing.
I'd lied when I'd said I was there to sightsee.
Now, I'm back here on the bridge's railing.
Alone, with no one coming to save me.

When I'm far away from home I think back,
to nights lying awake after bedtime.
Hearing your voice in the house was sublime.
Joking with mom and dad, telling wisecracks.
Smell of fresh baked cookies, cooling on racks.
Hoping maybe you'd stay longer this time.
We'd spend our days making art and bad rhymes.
Your guidance could have helped keep me on track.

But you didn't stay, the war needed men.
Wish you'd been there to stop me from leaving.
It's lonely here on this bleak mountain glen.
You're somewhere... miles from where I'm sleeping.
One day we'll reunite, don't know where or when.
Hope you still share laughter in the evening.

On the balcony, I watch leaves being blown.
A young woman emerges from next door.
The party she's escaped must be a bore.
For a moment she looks down at her phone.
She seems incurably sad and alone.
Inside, you can hear the party guests roar.
The girl is graceful, easy to fall for.
She leans on the rail, lets out a soft moan.

I stare out over the city below.
She's contemplating the same thing I am.
The nighttime streets are empty but aglow.
The easiest way out ends with a slam.
Our eyes soon meet and it's clear we both know.
Together and alone, soon to be damned.

Fran stood on the dock with flowers in hand.
Moments from now she would be face-to-face,
with the sailor she so longed to embrace.
He'd been off fighting in a foreign land,
but war was now over! Strike up the band!
Been so long though that her mind had misplaced,
what he looked like. O're time, he'd been effaced.
She fretted their date would not go as planned...

See, Fran could not recall if he was real,
or just someone she made up in her head.
Surviving the war had been an ordeal.
Maybe to stay calm each night in her bed,
did she just imagine a boyfriend ideal?
The gangplank descends and fills her with dread.

It's been almost (wait.. let's see) thirteen years,
since you passed away. I've always pondered...
Maybe you faked your own death and wandered
to the city you spoke of on the frontier.
Said you'd retire there after your career.
I live in that city now, have you not heard?
Traveled a thousand miles for reasons absurd.
I walk through its streets with eyes full of tears.

Nobody knows the true reason I moved.
Guess I hope I'll see you crossing the street.
And I'll shout, "Dad! See how much I've improved!"
He'll hug me tight and regret his deceit.
I know he's dead, but I should be excused.
I just miss him. Wish once more we could meet.

For now I'm young, but one day I'll grow old.
My face will change, and wrinkle, and turn gray.
Maybe I'll lose my hair, wear a toupee?
A cane, to walk steady, I'll have to hold.
And while my final fate still lies untold,
no matter how much I beg, plead, or pray,
whether by natural causes or foul play,
in due course, I'll stop moving and turn cold.

You'll never learn what happens to my face,
since you told me I'm no longer your beau.
Forever apart, separated by space.
Despite all you meant to me, I'll never know
the location of your final resting place,
or how your face has changed since this photo.

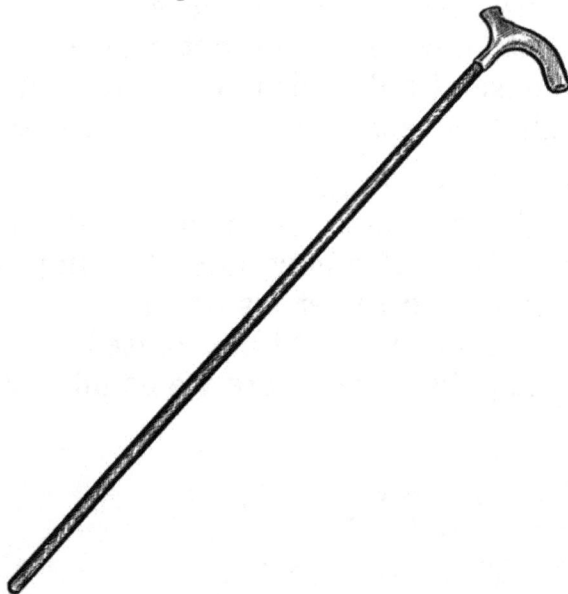

I never walked into that place again.
Too many ghosts at our favorite booth.
We ate there twice a week, back in our youth.
Sometimes just coffee, other times champagne.
Hours reading together, hiding from rain.
Sweet words over cocktails- gin and vermouth.
It's not those memories... I'll tell you the truth,
it's the front window's view of Elm St. and Main.

Where, even though there's no longer a trace,
not one drop of your blood on the asphalt,
I can't stop thinking 'bout your lovely face,
and the aftermath of that car's assault.
Just wish I could give you one last embrace,
and say the accident wasn't your fault.

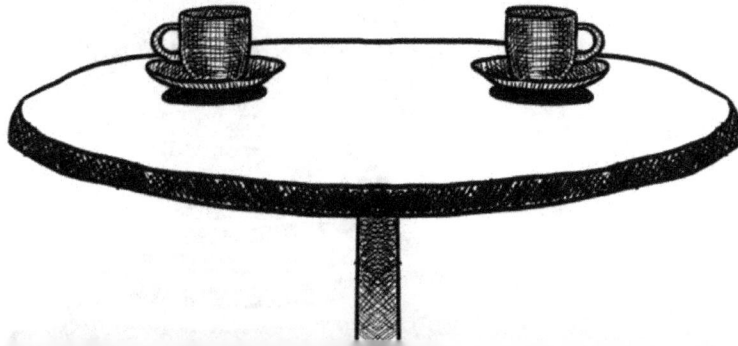

Saw a woman crying on the metro.
Everyone else just seemed to ignore her.
She softly wept tears she could not deter.
Had she been fired? A fight with her beau?
I felt bad and wished to comfort her woe.
She was alone with no one to confer.
But I'd say the wrong thing. She would demur.
I shouldn't feel guilty, should let it go.

But as her train sped off, I also wept.
Compassion inside, outside just a creep.
They were right about me, I'm too inept.
I get tongue-tied, it's not clear my soul's deep.
The fact I'm a monster I must accept.
A sad, lonely wolf, envious of sheep.

On the very last night of not knowing you,
we were two strangers who hadn't quite met.
But that brief intro was just the onset.
It didn't foretell what was to ensue.
Our casual friendship just grew and grew.
Then, on that footbridge, just after sunset...
You kissed me in a way I'll never forget.
We became lovers, moaning ahh! and ooh!

But soon we'd be more, dare I say, "soulmate?"
Two bodies, one soul, a single heartbeat.
Thought we'd soon wed... but that wasn't our fate.
It ended in fights, squabbles, and deceit.
We no longer speak or associate.
Strangers once more when we pass on the street.

When it's hard for you, remember these things;
Someone's kissing their baby for the first time.
And someone's eating yummy pie (key lime).
Someone's offering a box, tied up with string,
that holds a surprise engagement ring.
She's waited to say "yes" for a lifetime.
Someone bought a top-hat that's simply divine,
and just got the perfect haircut for Spring.

And you are alive and reading this verse.
And you'll be ok, I promise you that.
Sure, things could be better, but also worse.
One day you'll succeed and not just fall flat.
Ups and downs are part of the universe.
Cheer up, stop crying, quit being a brat.

I'll never fall in love completely,
The way it happens on the silver screen.
Like in the movies I'd watch as a teen,
where the leads match each other so neatly.
No one is out there who will "complete me."
One who will treat me like a king or queen.
Too much to expect they'll have good hygiene,
or ever talk to me gently and sweetly.

That sort of true love just does not exist.
At least not here in the real world, and yet...
Here you snore next to me after we've kissed,
ugly and hairy and covered in sweat.
And while you are a dumb, selfish, egoist,
it seems you're the best I'm going to get.

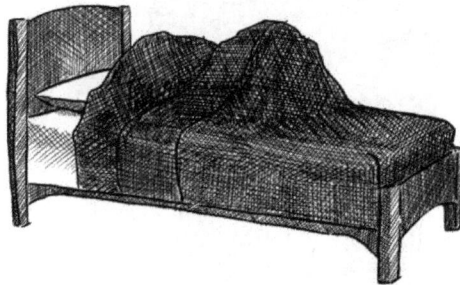

I love first times! Nothing else can compare.
Things are just better when they're unrehearsed.
No chocolate tastes as sweet as the first.
A horror film sequel just doesn't scare.
No romance can thrill like one's first affair.
My second draught just does not slack my thirst.
But as I get older, I feel like I'm cursed.
So much less is new. Naught but despair.

I've done it all. Nothing left to achieve.
Years since I've done something for the first time.
I'm old, wizened, grizzled, no longer naïve.
(It's even hard to think up a new rhyme...)
There's a fresh question I've begun to grieve–
"When did I first do something for the *last* time?"

Rue stared out the window at the city.
Millions of people there she didn't know.
A few of whom might someday be her beau.
One would be the person she would marry.
He was out there, completely unwary,
creating memories, both high and low,
that he would describe to her with gusto,
when she met him. He would be so witty!

So, don't fret when bad things happen to you.
Such tragedies always make for great tales,
and gives you a distinctive point of view,
that will impress Rue (and other females...).
You'll share with your grandkids all you went through.
Take good notes, don't forget any details.

Do you recall that first anniversary gift?
It was paper, as custom dictated.
Each year we're married, gifts get inflated.
Wouldn't want you to think that you'd been stiffed.
By year five, had to work an extra shift
(which is why your silver gift was belated)
Then gold for the tenth year we'd been mated.
Boy, the time sure does go by pretty swift...

If I could, I'd give you the whole planet!
I love you so much, my heart still goes boom!
And though I didn't have much time to plan it.
(Too many days spent in your hospital room...)
Guess this year, I'll make your gift of granite.
Something real nice to decorate your tomb.

Dear John,

This is where it's going to transpire...
We sit and sip coffee like nothing is wrong
pretending our love is still going strong.
Thoughts race through my brain, feels like it's on fire.
Hope I'll stay stoic, not be a crier.
You make small talk, and though I play along,
I know in my heart this is our swan song.
Wish this date could be like the ones' prior.

But this is the last time. Chances are slim
that we'll ever again meet face-to-face.
My lip quivers, hidden by the cup's rim.
Can't bear the thought that this is the last place,
I'll see you before you leave me for him.
I steel myself for your final embrace.

Almost every day, when I'm feeling bored,
I visit our town's magic library.
It does not house books of the ordinary,
but it's where tales never-written are stored.
There's a giant collection to be explored,
but I'm there for one reason primary.
I read accounts where I'm not solitary–
Biographies where our bond was restored.

I console myself reading love stories,
of how we're together and not apart.
They come in numerous categories,
and though some of it's trash, some is fine art.
Mostly it's yarns of our romantic glories.
They're all I have to soothe my broken heart.

Calmly walk 'cross the room towards your front door.
Do not give away the tiniest clue,
of what it is that you intend to do.
Try to not make a sound, or you're done for.
Put out of your mind all that came before.
Turn the knob gently, without a miscue.
Step over the threshold. Now you are through.
Don't turn around, even if they implore.

Don't ever look back. Break into a run.
Keep running and running (don't walk briskly)
Too dangerous to stop once you've begun.
Get to the dock, take a boat 'cross the sea.
In that new land, you'll be known by no one.
You'll never be found. You are finally free.

I was finally ready to begin—
To journey down into that hidden cave,
an underground, dinosaur-people enclave.
Pistols ready for the danger within.
Glowing fungi, blind beasts with pale white skin.
Though there'd be adventure, risks, and close shaves...
Not the least bit frightened. I'm really brave!
Know how to brawl, even with my weak chin.

The pangs in my heart came not from worry
about any dangers that might ensue.
But I'd planned... (excuse me... eyes wet and blurry...)
to abandon the surface world *with you*.
Instead, I'm escaping the memory
of losing your love to that ingenue.

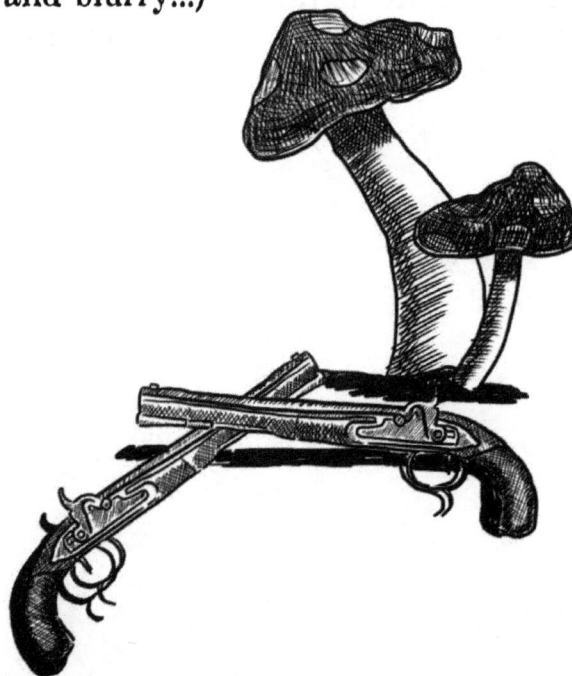

Scienza

Scien

Scienza

cienza

Scienza

Scienza

Scienza

Scienza

Scienza

Scienza

I know that you came here looking for verse.
But I must talk about math; fractals in fact.
Which are small things holding big things, compact.
Now math's a subject to which I'm adverse,
I don't know much, so I'll try to be terse...
If you have a giant thing (in the abstract),
each small piece contains the full thing intact.
Thus a sand grain holds the whole universe.

So, in theory, a study of this single grain,
might provide the answers to set me free.
Every action that's been, all the joy and the pain,
once hidden from view will be plain to see.
And when I relive it all once again,
I'll know what I did that made you leave me.

Smart men in lab coats with fancy degrees,
have spent long years studying outer space.
Discovering black holes at a rapid pace.
I've been keeping up on all their decrees.
If you get close, you'll start to get squeezed.
Any information is then erased.
All that goes in is forever misplaced.
A scary thought, though one that makes me most pleased.

Had an idea, finally had me a goal.
And I got to work, I kept going full tilt.
Something that could fix my tormented soul.
If I could just get this damn rocketship built.
I'd fly straight on up and into that hole,
and irreversibly rid myself of this guilt.

In the fullness of time, the sun will burst.
The stars will collide, or burn out and fade.
Galaxies will lose form; orbits degrade.
And, unless the arrow of time is reversed,
all the atoms in space will be dispersed.
Eventually (even if long delayed),
every proton that's left will have decayed.
So goes the heat death of the universe.

But here on this bleak Earth, time ticks by slow.
No people or trees, just dust and dry stone.
The last living thing died some ages ago.
I'm all that's left– a forlorn ghost, alone.
I wait, bored senseless. For how long? I don't know.
With no one to haunt, or way to atone.

"Dear Sir, we've been up here for some weeks now,
and we can't seem to find the ground anymore.
The wild blue yonder we'd sought to explore,
but the blimp's flown too high, I've no idea how.
Our engineers don't possess the knowhow
to navigate back down to field or shore.
Send assistance, I beg, plead, and implore!"
The man swigged his last draught of curaçao.

Then he rolled up the short, handwritten note,
stuffed it in the bottle to keep it dry.
He knew chance for rescue might be remote,
but off the gondola he let it fly.
And watched and prayed with a lump in his throat,
as it fell into an azure-blue sky.

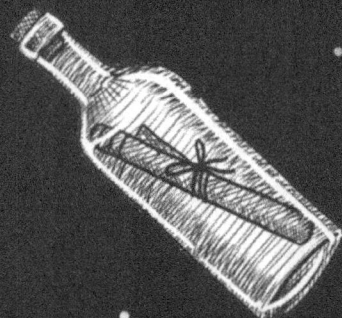

I bought my time machine to get away,
from this wretched present, to a new time.
To a future filled with things in their prime,
since "now" is naught but gloomy, dull, and gray.
Behind me was the sad world of "today."
The land of idiots, hunger, and crime.
Turns out, the future was less than sublime.
Not one soul was there, could it be foul play?

Silence, the only thing left. This was bad!
And no matter how far ahead I combed,
I could not locate a single comrade.
Empty time machine boxes sat in each home.
Seems they all had the same thought as I'd had,
and into *their* future, they also did roam.

On the skyline, smoke and souls, mushroom cloud,
can still be seen rising into the sky.
No explanation. No reason for why.
A flash, a hot wind, and a noise so loud,
suddenly blew past the unwary crowd.
There was not any time for a last goodbye,
just the distant, faint sound of a child's cry.
A layer of ash blankets like a shroud.

Things are quiet and peaceful here miles away,
as the snow gently falls on the unburied dead.
Under a bleak sky, now gun-metal gray,
bodies litter the streets, wounded have fled.
A press release declares, in words, cliché,
"Success!" by those proud of their new warhead.

If you travel faster than light, you can,
in theory reverse the arrow of time.
Although I've grown old and way past my prime,
I have at long last completed my plan–
To build a finely-tuned receiver and,
rocket to the proper place in spacetime,
where transmissions sent ages ago now align.
And once more I hear your voice on my scan...

Among the stars I listen to our talk.
"I love you," you said (you said it a lot).
But to my proposal you chose to balk.
Though it was years ago, my insides grow taut,
as I hear, "I can't be yours in wedlock,"
And I cry once again, my heart in a knot.

There are a lot of things that totally suck
'bout being attacked by space invaders.
At first, we hoped they were peaceful traders....
But our cities they began to destruct,
and our young women they sought to abduct.
Yep, these guys were truly nasty raiders.
And now they rule Earth as vile dictators.
But in one strange aspect, we were in luck...

You see, before they came we were alone.
It was just us, no one else was out there.
But when the cruel spacemen made themselves known,
we could stop being lonely, full of despair.
And as a species, I think that we've grown,
by seeing a sample to which we could compare.

Robot X-5 saw M-9 from afar.
Falling for her was not what was planned.
But he felt that their romance would be grand.
Maybe you think such a thing is bizarre...
But he courted her, strumming a guitar.
And while he knew robot love had been banned,
he said, "M-9, I want to touch your hand,
and feel my heart explode like a new star!"

Romantics would say that what occurred next,
was true love that refused to play by laws.
Scientists who spent time reviewing the specs,
found plutonium cores to be the cause.
T'was critical mass, and physics complex.
Two hearts, too close, blew up due to their flaws.

When you announce you've built a time machine,
all your friends will suggest places to go.
"A trip to dark ages, long, long ago?"
"Journey back to guide yourself as a teen?"
A few may hint about something obscene,
or say, "place sports bets, pay back what you owe."
Mostly they hope I'll use guns and ammo
to kill baby Hitler, wipe the slate clean.

And I know, those are all great ideas, sure.
But that's not why I crafted my device.
I have an objective that's much more pure.
Just have to relive, at least once or twice,
that last perfect day from the time before...
To see you one more time, I'd pay any price.

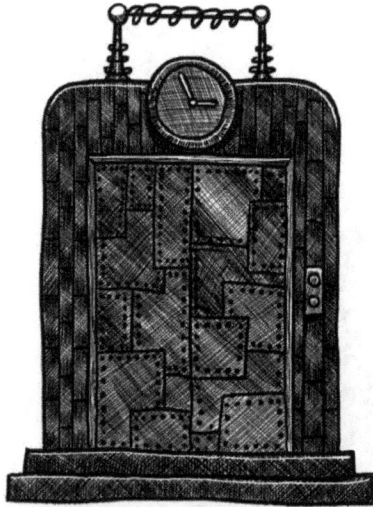

The weird mailman handed Jim the letter.
Inside was a precious, handwritten note,
penned by the girl on which he once did dote.
She'd spurned his love; he'd tried to forget her,
so this new missive made his eyes wetter.
He quickly read her words and anecdotes.
But strange spelling errors soon did denote,
t'was not for him. He should have known better.

Postal error. Meant for a parallel world.
Misdirected in the dimensional flow.
To a duplicate Jim from a duplicate girl.
Guess on that Earth she'd said "yes" not "no."
He felt so loved but also not at all.
Alone here; but somewhere, he was her beau.

When I was small, I learned this world was plain.
Nothing magical; just physics, just math.
There's no sea monster lurking in my bath.
The only way to fly was by airplane.
I went to school to develop my brain.
A science PhD would be my path!
Resigned to never face a dragon's wrath,
or raise the dead with spells, dark and arcane.

Then one day I allowed myself to dream.
Saw the cosmos with more than just my eye.
Soon I designed weird guns to shoot ray-beams,
rode a unicorn that also could fly,
traveled space and time, both down and upstream,
and wrote dumb poems that don't really rhyme.

We stood on roofs in pjs and winter coats,
the night the queer spaceships filled our skies.
Our history books we'd have to revise,
to assess what alien life did denote.
We waited for contact... lumps in our throats.
Unsure if they'd be enemies or allies?
We could do scant more than guess or surmise.
They just sat silent, continued to float.

Three days later they left, never to return.
They left without saying a single word.
Years later, their rejection still does burn.
What could it be? Was it something they heard?
We've been introspecting, in order to learn,
what on our world made them find us absurd?

About a million, billion years ago,
and a million, billion miles away,
out of a giant star some photons did spray.
A fusion reaction caused quite a glow,
that shot off at light-speed (which is not slow).
By the time the photons had reached halfway,
they'd red-shifted to visible light from x-ray,
only to stop here, on my patio.

Light born long ago in that long-dead star,
started a journey that ends with my eye.
Welcome light ray, I know you've traveled far.
It's a warm summer night here in July.
Let me play you a song on my guitar,
and appreciate the fact you've dropped by.

Our top scientists made a new germ.
The only cure was to fall madly in love.
Truly, deeply in love, not just "sort of."
T'was eugenics meant to cull not the infirm,
but to euthanize those lonely bookworms.
The approval came from those up above,
who felt that our culture needed a shove.
A harsh solution. But good in long-term...

Those who don't find mates are doubtless insane.
Without true love, life's not worth existing.
Perhaps the virus was more than humane.
Most went to their graves barely resisting.
The lonely are no longer here to complain,
or bum us out 'stead of being uplifting.

I had my genes spliced with a tardigrade,
so I'd survive in the vacuum of space.
In a block of ice, I could be encased,
and I'd come out just fine. I'm not afraid.
Can't be killed by bullets, bombs, or grenades.
DNA's too strong for x-rays to displace.
My lungs laugh at poisons, nerve gas, and mace.
Yup, it was certainly quite the upgrade!

There's only one thing I could not survive–
You walking away would make my heart break.
I need your love, I'll perish if deprived.
This new monster body... was a mistake.
Seems my eight, stubby legs killed your sex drive.
The disgust in your eyes makes my claws quake.

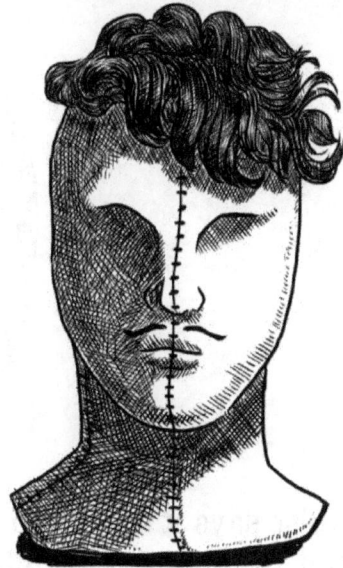

A shrewd inventor invented a glue.
Wasn't designed for a cracked mug or plate,
wouldn't help keep your toupee on straight,
but would mend a broken heart, good as new.
To buy it, people lined up in a queue!
Quite useful after a real bad first date,
or following the death of your soulmate.
But I'm afraid its aid, I must eschew.

Even though your rejection hurt me real bad,
I can't bear to quickly get over you.
Oft' when things end, it makes sense to feel sad
(even though the tears use up all my tissues).
One day I'll look back at "us" and be glad.
The loss gives our time together value.

My therapist says it's time to move on.
No amount of remorse can change the past.
Says I should cheer up, stop being downcast.
Need to look forward, not be so withdrawn.
But my mind is stuck back in that salon,
with the things I said that left you aghast.
So awful that you walked away at last.
"Too late now to fix it. Those days are gone."

I think that she's wrong though, and I'll tell you why...
I have a time-machine powered by guilt.
While I know the first time things went awry,
once I finally finish getting it built,
and work up some more shame, I'll go retry,
to prevent your love from starting to wilt.

The roads of the town are empty and dead.
Street lights perform without any drivers.
None left alive. There are no survivors.
Did not matter that they begged and they pled.
All from that device I built in my shed.
(Yes... I'm this Armageddon's deviser.)
Dear Bea is lifeless, I can't revive her.
Why didn't she listen to what I said?

I only crafted this doomsday machine
as a cry for help. You should have stopped me.
I just craved respect, wanted to be seen.
Why didn't you notice and stop me Bea?
You were supposed to arrive on the scene
just in time and change my mind with your plea.

This is my farewell transmission from Mars.
My batteries are starting to run low.
The lights in my eyes will no longer glow.
Not much time left to compose my memoirs.
But thanks for rocketing me out to the stars.
I'm sending you all one final photo.
It's now sunset here. The sky's all aglow.
Congrats on your mission. Light up your cigars!

Remember I love you, and I agree,
makes sense to use 'bots to explore the unknown.
So take this... as a request, not a plea.
I'll be here patiently waiting, alone.
Hoping someday you'll fly up and get me;
dust me off, charge me up, and take me home.

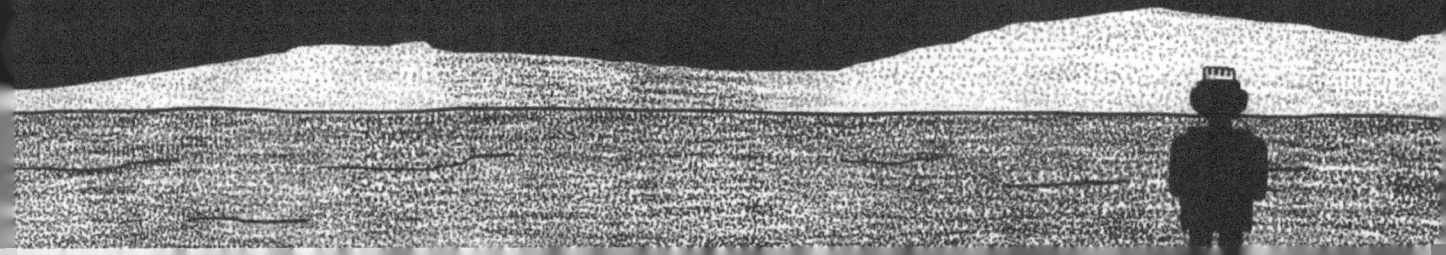

O're the years I've invented lots of stuff;
Spaceships to take you to Mars really fast.
Robots that make perfect weather forecasts.
Lockpicks to get out of any handcuffs.
But these days I'm lonely and bored enough,
to work on this new invention at last;
"A mailbox that sends letters to the past."
While I admit, my plans are a bit rough,

I've plenty of time, (though not much support).
But if I make calculations precise,
I'm sure I can cause space-time to distort.
I'll then write a note to myself, concise,
and tell past-me something of great import–
"Please don't invent that damn doomsday device!"

Raising good kids these days is such a chore.
There's always tantrums, major and minor.
You hope they'll grow up gentler and kinder,
but they end up writhing around on the floor,
and embarrassing us both at the store.
My child's turned into such a whiner.
To set her straight, I had to remind her,
that she wasn't a little girl anymore...

But just a sophisticated machine,
programmed to believe it was a young lass,
to replace my real child who died as a teen.
So if she kept on being such an ass,
I'd give up and wipe her memory clean,
trade her in for a model with less sass.

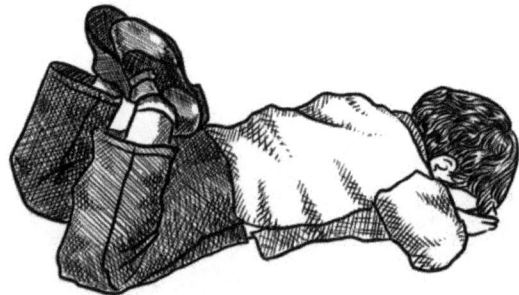

To the bold crew of mighty Ulysses,
left adrift on waves returning from Troy.
To sailors sunk in Magellan's employ.
To brave Amelia, vanished o're the seas.
Doomed Arctic explorers starting to freeze.
Colonists vanished from Martian convoys.
And Captain Zod– interstellar envoy,
whose spaceship flew off course... a few degrees.

We know you're all out there, we know you are lost.
We can't bear to leave you to fates unknown.
We've plans for a ship and time-machine, crossed,
designed to fly through spacetime's quantum foam.
We're going to build it, at any cost,
and we will find a way to bring you home.

Even though it had been many long years,
she knows not a single day will pass by,
when he won't think of her. Want to know why?
That he'd forget wasn't one of her fears,
'cause his starship had lost one of its gears,
and straight into a black hole he did fly.
Time, the event horizon does defy.
Seconds stretched to eons as he disappears.

His last thoughts as he falls into that hole,
will stay static until the end of time.
A smeared out message to mission control...
"Tell Amanda I love her and that I'm..."
Eternal love is every lovers' goal–
Their love would always be trapped in its prime.

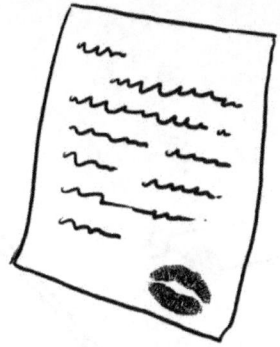

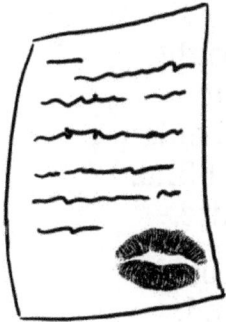

There'll never be another "you and I..."
But that doesn't mean I will be alone,
since I've a device that can make a clone.
Parts of "us" that went bad, I'd just retry.
Thought, "this will end well, what could go awry?"
But each new version of "you" made me groan—
Treated me bad or wore too much cologne.
Was wrong to think a better you would come by.

Guess I'm saying... what we had was unique,
and can't be replicated by science.
That robot you've replaced me with is a freak!
It's not a girlfriend, just an appliance.
This high-tech future is nothing but bleak.
Let's dump our toys and renew our alliance.

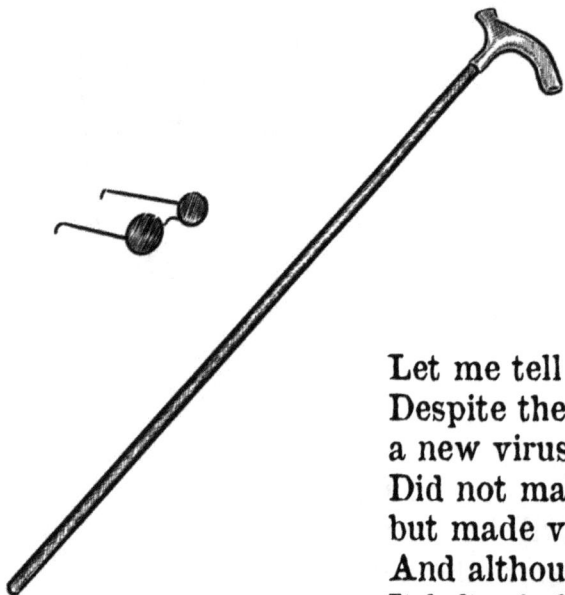

Let me tell you the story of our plight...
Despite the fact we were all quarantined,
a new virus infected all mankind.
Did not make you cough, or kill you outright,
but made victims fall in love at first sight.
And although that sounds like it's more benign,
It left wholly immune those whom were blind.
The plague could not compel them to unite.

We gave them our love, they didn't love back.
Were loyal and true, they jerked us around.
They were our full meal, we were but a snack.
They ignored our requests to settle down.
Volunteers for their harems they do not lack.
All of us waiting in our wedding gowns.

Racca-
pricci-
ante

Darling, my love for you is oh so strong.
I can't help but be true, I'll never stray.
On your pillow, my head will always lay.
If made to leave, I'll be back before long.
I can't help but love how we get along.
(I'm sorry, I know that that sounds cliché.)
I'll be here next week and also today.
I don't think you can do anything wrong!

So... I'm hurt that you've hired a few exorcists,
priests, shamans, monks, and some crazed voodoo queen.
You keep asserting you don't think I exist,
and frankly my dear, that's a little bit mean.
Nothing in creation could make me desist...
Not since losing my head to that guillotine.

I come to on a lonely road, driving.
Must have zoned out for a few minutes there.
Seems I'm still in the middle of nowhere.
Don't know how many hours 'til I'm arriving.
A thought occurs to me, one that's surprising—
Perhaps I crashed miles back there somewhere?
Did I die? The idea makes me despair.
My soul never resting, just reviving.

I come to on a lonely road, driving.
Must have zoned out for a few minutes there.
A thought occurs to me, one that's surprising—
Perhaps I crashed miles back there somewhere?
My soul never resting, just reviving,
again and again, in the cool night air.

"Oh hey, it's you," I awoke with a start.
Remember the day that we fell in love?
Or that morning picnic amongst the foxglove?
The night at the opera when you won my heart?
The months during the war we spent apart?
The time at the lake feeding geese and doves?
And, not to forget what I'm most proud of...
In front of a priest swore, "'til death do us part."

That last one's important 'cause, as I've said,
my love only lasts as long as that vow.
You fell off a tall horse and hit your head.
I was devastated, but anyhow...
Honey, please realize that for months you've been dead!
So sorry, it's time for you to go now.

Deep under the soil, right beneath your feet,
lives an underground race with not much luck.
They toil in darkness and dirt and in muck,
living lives of despair, sorrow replete.
But now and again they earn a small treat–
They poke through their roof, find themselves awestruck
at the view of our sky. Their eyes get stuck.
Yet frightened of beauty, they soon retreat.

For to those souls our world is but a dream.
Seems like a heaven, rapture, paradise.
What we view as normal, just simple, mainstream,
they see as lavish to the point of vice.
There is divinity in a sunbeam.
So value mother Earth, don't just say it's "nice."

Clinics are not a place for the occult.
Learned nurses attend those brides and grooms,
tensely gathered in delivery rooms.
Nearby, doctors observe, prepared to consult.
The child's first cry is the greatest result!
Once born, the staff leaves, or so you'd assume....
But soon a weird man garbed in strange costume
sneaks into the ward, seen by no adult.

He's tall, lanky, queer, and festooned with gears.
As mom sleeps, he creeps in with a weird gait,
and he whispers odd things in each child's ears.
What he says is never up for debate.
But it can bring joy or bring them to tears,
as he describes to each young babe their fate.

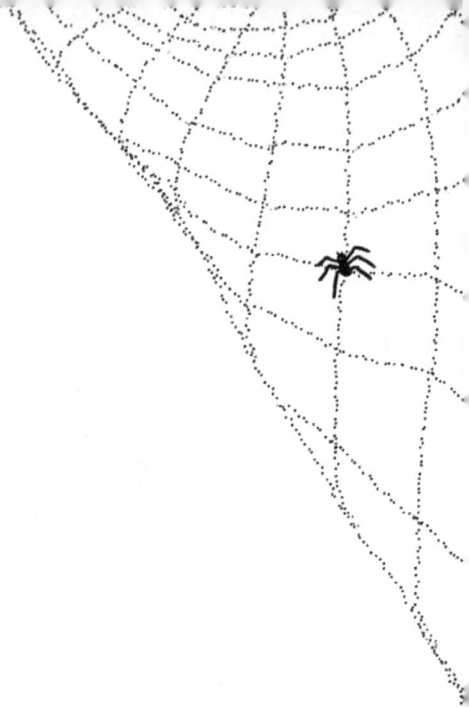

Welcome my child to my scenic chateau!
Your room's ready. I've had time to prepare.
Improved it from the standard witch's lair–
Swept the cobwebs out of every shadow.
Shooed all the swamp monsters from the grotto.
Removed vile beasties that would give you scares.
Nothing is left that could cause you nightmares.
Not a thing to be worried about... although...

If you happen to hear an odd scratching noise,
that from behind the basement stairs comes up,
just try to ignore it, play with your toys.
Don't call for exorcists, priests, or bishops.
No need to lose control, just keep your poise.
It's just what I use to cure my hiccups.

Glum men in green wool coats boarded the train.
A young bride in tears, eyes filled with concern,
shouted to her soldier, "I already yearn!
I refuse to never see you again...
Promise me that no matter what the pain,
no matter the cost, for me you'll return!"
He made that vow, as the engine did churn,
"No matter what, I'll come back to you, Jane."

Days, weeks, and months went by with nary a word.
She lay in bed sobbing, no one to hold.
One night in the darkness, shambling was heard...
A scent in the air of fresh earth and mold.
She grinned, (and I know this may sound absurd),
he'd kept his vow, though now scary and cold.

Though it's serene here in this calm graveyard,
in dim tunnels six feet beneath the soil,
a host of pale, ghoulish workers do toil,
bringing coffins downward to their dark lord.
Through black idols, dreadful gods guide their horde,
to a place so hot it'd make your blood boil.
Newly buried are best, before they spoil.
Young, firm flesh tastes better than old and scarred.

But try not to let that ruin our picnic.
They likely can't hear you up here anyway.
Don't let the thought of those beasts make you sick.
Laugh, joke, love, and live, be happy and gay.
Sure, if they grab you, your death won't come quick.
But until then, have a happy birthday!

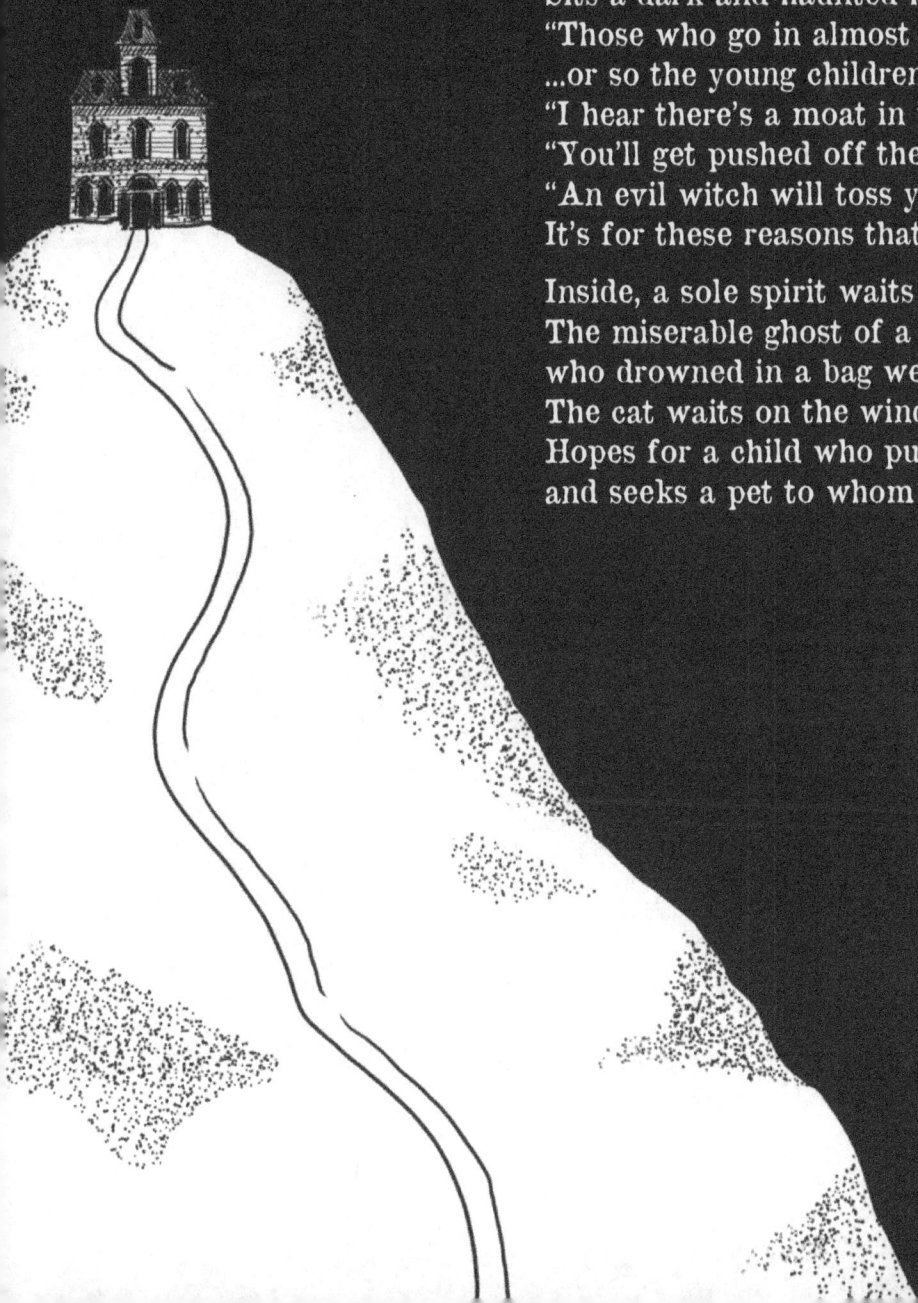

On a dark hill on the outskirts of town,
Sits a dark and haunted house, painted black.
"Those who go in almost never come back."
...or so the young children oft' say with a frown.
"I hear there's a moat in which you could drown!"
"You'll get pushed off the roof; your head will crack!"
"An evil witch will toss you in a sack!"
It's for these reasons that none will go 'round.

Inside, a sole spirit waits all alone.
The miserable ghost of a small kitten,
who drowned in a bag weighted down with a stone.
The cat waits on the window sill, sittin',
Hopes for a child who pursues the unknown,
and seeks a pet to whom they'll be smitten.

I hate being the guy on watch at night.
Roar of unseen waves on the dark ocean,
stomach's all nauseous from the sea's motion,
but worst of all is that damn ghostly light.
Bobbing behind us, at the edge of sight.
Never closes in, or causes commotion,
but what it could be...? Don't have a notion.
It creeps me the hell out, chills me with fright.

Once dawn starts to break, it is always gone.
Is it waiting for a time opportune?
Captain's seen it, but insists we press on.
So I spend each watch clutching my harpoon,
risking my life for silks and cardamon.
This voyage is cursed. Pray we reach land soon.

It took many years of effort and work.
Getting that private island he'd dreamed of.
To get this far, others he'd had to shove...
Stuff he did might make you think him a jerk,
but an island retreat was quite a perk.
Along the way he had lost his true love,
but of such concerns he was now above.
He stared at the sunset, mouth in a smirk.

On this island he now felt like a lord.
He hoped and prayed this watery divide,
would keep him safe from the large zombie horde,
that was now roaming 'cross the countryside.
He poured some wine just because he was bored,
then shed one last tear for those who had died.

This is the store where I bought the suitcase,
that would one day hold my cold, severed head.
Got it just before I was to be wed;
a honeymoon, a kiss, a warm embrace.
T'wasn't the fancy kind, just commonplace.
Figured I'd save cash for my bride instead.
Boy, let me tell you, her plans I misread!
The outside was leather, the lining lace.

I chose that bag because it was light blue,
and had a compartment for my passport.
It was waterproof– good for the canoe,
that would take us to the jungle resort.
Never suspected dark rites and voodoo,
were being plotted by my sweet consort.

On a moonless night, in a forest wild,
a young woman, alone, digs a small grave.
Just a simple hole, no slab to engrave.
No threnody sung, no stones are piled.
She hopes this makeshift tomb won't be defiled.
The task complete, she leaves without a wave.
Not one tear... is she trying to be brave?
No mom should have to bury their own child.

"Just an unmarked grave in a potters' field.
That kid deserved something much less shoddy."
"But," she knows, "this is where he must stay sealed,"
although the crypt is gross, damp, and soddy.
How else could she keep his murder concealed,
so that nosy sheriff won't find the body?

Five hundred miles of mountains and ice,
kept our arctic village safe from the dead,
who rose out of graves and began to spread,
after a lab chose the wrong gene to splice.
Our frosty haven was secure and nice,
but as we pondered the long night ahead,
we were filled with fear, despair, and dread.
No zombie horde, left to our own device.

Radios went silent three days 'fore sunset.
We stood on the beach and wondered what's next?
Sure, we were secure from the undead threat,
but now we were burdened, troubled, and vexed.
Obligations started to make us sweat.
Rebuilding the world is a task too complex.

It's well known that for your wish to come true,
when making a wish at a wishing well,
a thing of value is key to the spell.
Can't toss in some rubbish or an old gym shoe.
It requires a gold coin (or a whole slew!)
The sacrifice has to be something swell,
from one who seeks the spirits to compel,
into granting a wish with their voodoo.

And so, though I stand in waist-deep water,
I'm finally certain I have some worth!
My Mom and Dad must have loved their daughter
(It's something I've fretted about since birth)
Spell would fail if they hadn't adored her.
That's why they threw me down into the earth.

I'm not sure that I know where to begin...
Guess it started with no more than a hunch.
Perhaps a strange comment one day at brunch?
But something changed from the way it had been.
My spouse now leers at me with a sly grin,
and each morn declares he loves me a bunch.
So I spied on him one day after lunch...
Caught a beast putting on my husband's skin!

That finally explains his sudden caprice.
At first I was shocked, but now quite torn.
I must admit, the beast's been much more nice.
Doesn't yell or scream or treat me with scorn.
Yup, this murderous fiend is worth the price.
I'll stick with the beast, no reason to mourn.

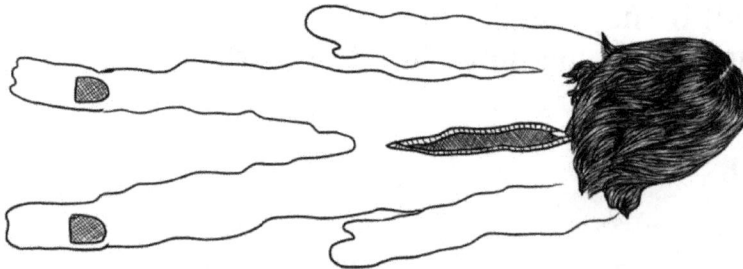

The first thing Charlotte felt as she awoke,
was soft, warm breath on the back of her neck.
Moist lips close enough to give her a peck.
Arm held her tight, much too gentle to choke.
In her chest, feelings began to evoke...
Fog of sleep lifted, she thought, "what the heck?!?"
Meant just one thing, she did not have to check.
It had happened once more, t'was not a joke.

The beast from the basement escaped again.
The pits and traps it managed to defeat.
Looks like it would take stronger locks and chains,
to keep the rotten thing out of her suite.
It'll take hours to stuff it back down the drain,
and once done she'd still have to wash the sheet.

Isaac was so eager to start haunting
the people who moved in after he died.
His house'd been bought by a young groom and bride.
"How dare they!" he thought, planning on taunting.
(Though it was clear, he'd left the place wanting.)
The couple cleaned and scrubbed the whole inside.
All the rugs were shampooed, paint was applied.
Did every task Isaac had found daunting.

Patched the leaky roof, refinished the floors,
spent nights with their children, to whom they read.
Planted a garden, hung bird feeders outdoors.
Isaac soon realized he'd been a blockhead.
He left a sweet note saying, "This place is yours!"
Gave up haunting, baked them cookies instead.

You should give careful consideration,
instead of blurting out your very first thought,
when a genie's magic lamp you have bought.
I didn't. And to my consternation,
regret not putting in more cogitation.
(I could have asked to be an astronaut!)
But "eternal life" was the wish that I sought.
Centuries later, this revelation—

All of your true loves will someday be lost.
Countless funerals you'll have to attend.
Thrills become dull when there's no risk or cost.
You'll dwell on mistakes far too late to mend.
All routes to happiness you will exhaust,
but your regrets stay with you to the end.

At that strange circus on the outskirts of town,
a peculiar tent has a peculiar sign.
"To Heaven," it says in one handwritten line.
Inside is a single, peculiar clown,
and a ladder up to a door painted brown.
Through the door's cracks you can see something shine.
And while people seem to think it's benign,
those that go up... never ever come down.

Heaven's a great place, if I've understood.
So if they're happy there, guess I'll be glad.
But... seems like some would come back if they could.
Maybe they're trapped in that evil doodad!
So, I guess it must lead to somewhere good,
or else it leads somewhere extremely bad...

Malvagita

The way genetics works is pretty weird.
In my mirror are two different faces—
both of my parents, my visage encases.
Each left something in me to be revered,
mashed into one person; identities smeared.
Her nose, his eyes, lots of other traces...
I had Mom's buckteeth (before I got braces),
with Dad's coal-black hair and thin, wispy beard.

Thought they'd be a couple for my whole life.
...I guess I wasn't a strong enough tether.
'cause they fought and fought, there was so much strife.
The marital stress they could not weather.
It ended badly, via sharp kitchen knife.
On my face, at least, they're still together.

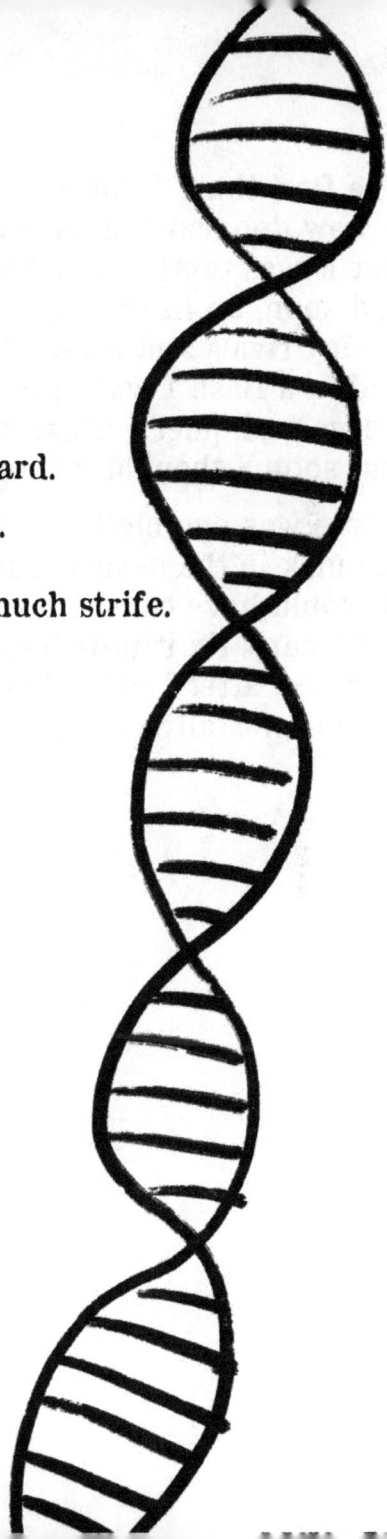

The first thing I did was read the manual.
A new doomsday device is not a toy!
But it was pretty clear how to employ,
and soon, up in the sky went the bombshell...
To my rivals and foes, I bade farewell,
and in a flash I was alone, oh boy!
Peace and quiet I began to enjoy.
But soon a thought hit, one that made me unwell.

There was one big flaw they'd failed to mention...
A quirk in the design that's built-in.
It would have caused me some apprehension,
but I can't fix it now (much to my chagrin).
You see, after I used this invention...
no one was alive to forgive my sin.

Those that take note of the half-full wine glass,
hold a view that they have a wonderous life.
Love a gorgeous groom (or beautiful wife).
Undaunted by tests– sure they'll always pass.
Gloomy ones see a half-empty wine glass.
'round each corner lurks a thug with a knife.
Challenges everywhere, days full of strife.
No victories; everything's an impasse.

I see a cup neither empty nor full,
when I'm trying to choose which glass to pick.
I find sophistry unbearably dull.
Don't care if the brew's too thin or too thick.
The only question o're which I'll oft' mull,
is if there's enough poison to do the trick.

When I was small, I was naught but a fool.
Didn't know better, an innocent child.
Never heeded my elders, just ran wild.
One spring day, I almost drowned in the pool.
Woke up coughing, my face covered in drool.
And while police wrote reports to be filed,
relieved teachers, family, and friends just smiled.
"Luckily saved from a fate all too cruel!"

But was I lucky? I'm not all too sure.
As I grew, I became more and more vile.
With each new crime, I was less and less pure.
My once virtuous soul I began to defile.
A naïve child's path to heaven's secure,
while sinners like me face a fiery trial.

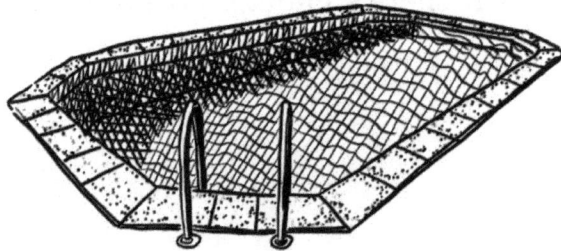

Ever since the time we said our goodbye,
that warm summer day, out by the lake house.
(I still recall the color of your blouse.)
As you spilled your plan, all I did was cry.
I get your point... you needed a fall guy.
And while I had hoped you'd soon be my spouse,
I did not say a word, quiet as a mouse.
Soon you were off to find an alibi.

I've done what I can to stay close to you,
because you were what gave my life purpose.
On warm summer days, you ride your canoe,
you get a chill, and start looking nervous.
You stare at the lake, I know that you do.
Trying hard to see me from the surface.

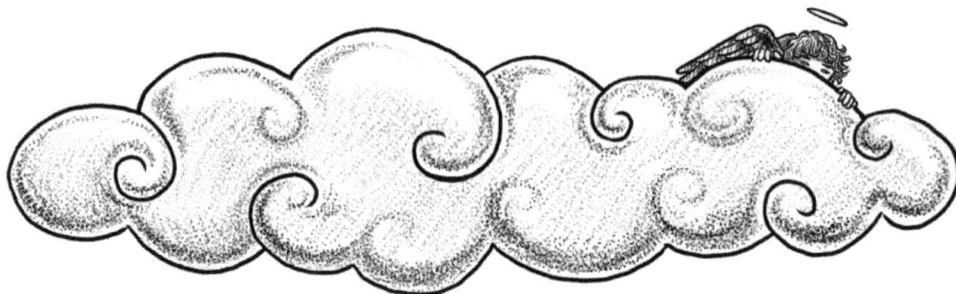

I was a scoundrel, of that I'll admit.
More than a scoundrel, a real evil fiend.
From a young age, on misdeeds I'd been weaned.
But for virtuous Ann... evil I quit.
Not one more bad act I swore to commit!
For I knew when I died, I would be screened
by the angels, so my soul must be cleaned.
Else they'd not let me in, find me unfit.

When I died, I thought in heaven we'd meet.
But I found out a fact I wish I'd had known.
Ann assumed to hell my soul would retreat,
so she killed some kids, and did not atone.
She wasn't in heaven for me to greet.
We both spent the long afterlife alone.

When I met you, my head started to spin.
Soon after that though, you first made me cry.
Never told the truth, all you did was lie.
Nothing more than an abusive has-been.
The scars you left on my porcelain skin,
are all I have to remember you by.
No photos or fond words, just a black eye.
Well, there is one thing that still makes me grin...

When it became clear you would not repent,
and I had you murdered by a cut-throat,
I made sure to get a large settlement.
The insurance made my bank account bloat!
And now for each single dollar that's spent,
I take a second, think of you, and gloat.

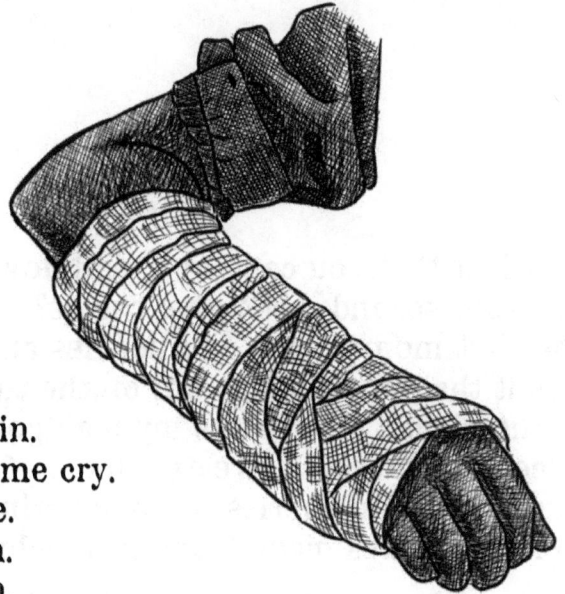

Why is it that you can never nail down,
that split second when love begins?
(the first moment you felt needles and pins?)
Was it that glorious day out on the town?
Or the night I let you see my nightgown...
'tween the sheets, a sweaty bundle of limbs?
So many fun memories, so many grins.
So many smiles made from upside-down frowns.

Can't really say when I first fell in love.
But I do know exactly when it ended.
I asked if you loved me, you said, "sort-of."
You didn't get why I was offended.
So at this cliff's edge I gave you a shove.
My love for you died as you descended.

LAST WILL & TESTAMENT

Mother told me you were a no-good lout.
Such a disreputable character!
"Find a better man– a doctor or barrister."
But darlin', never had the slightest doubt.
From the first glance, I knew to ask you out.
Must say... your wickedness was a factor.
You helped to throw Mom under a tractor.
The accomplice I could not do without!

And now, despite Mom's loud protestation,
you've made me a very wealthy heiress.
But dear, it's time we end our flirtation.
A low-class groom would make me embarrassed.
So I'll bury your corpse on my plantation,
and wed that tycoon who says I'm the fairest.

How did I become such a great villain?
It certainly wasn't my parent's fault.
Never taught to kill or rob a bank vault.
Unlike me, they were strictly civilians.
The true reason this kid grew reptilian,
and too strong for any hero to halt?
It's from enduring assault after assault.
Fought a hundred battles... No! A million!

T'was all those meddlers travelling through time.
Coming back to stop me from growing up.
Every jerk with a time machine thought it sublime
to plant bombs in my crib or poison my cup.
Fending them off made me flawless at crime,
...and gave me my psychopathic hang-ups.

I figured waiting in line was a waste.
Santa wouldn't give me what I *really* want.
All these kids were seeking new toys to flaunt.
My wish was of a more "peculiar" taste.
But I got on his fat lap, all red-faced.
Let's get this over. Mom waits with my aunt.
Once done, we'll eat in some dumb restaurant.
Santa leaned in close, with hand on my waist.

"Ho Ho Ho," he whispered, "No problem, child."
"I'm a bona-fide Santa, not some jackass.
I'll admit your Christmas wish is quite wild.
But you were good all year, never missed class.
Just leave the back door unlocked," he smiled,
"...and place a sharp knife next to the milk glass."

I dreamt of you again in bed last night.
We were at a vineyard drinking fine wines.
Night before, I dreamt we strolled through the pines.
I'm sure this eve we'll again reunite.
All week now, when to my bed I alight,
you've been waiting... whispering pick-up lines.
So obvious, no one could miss the signs.
Why don't you understand that this ain't right?

How many times have I said, "leave me alone!"
My dreams are *my* dreams. Don't need a director.
Your intrusion's not a thing I condone.
Knock it off with that damn psychic projector!
Do it again and I'll pick up the phone,
and report you to the police inspector.

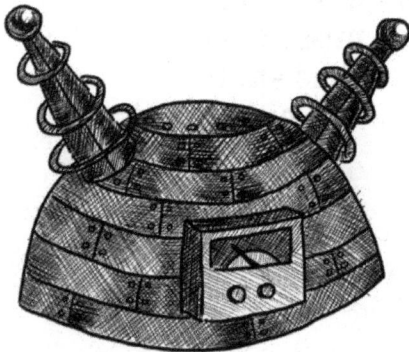

In the many worlds of the multiverse,
it's clear we're in an abandoned timeline.
A dead-end Earth, ignored by things divine.
Been forsaken by God, this place is cursed.
Our prayers unanswered; we get the inverse,
and society continues to decline.
Unjustly neglected in the grand design.
It's not fair at all. It's frankly perverse.

So we're building a door to a new place.
A world where "you" and "I" are both better.
I'll find that Earth's "me," punch him in the face,
drive his car, spend his cash, wear his sweater.
I'll date his girl, who's like *you*... but with grace.
You can have *him*, who, unlike me, pens love letters.

I liked to tell people I'd been misled,
but honestly, I was a vile brute.
From the start, I furthered my ill-repute.
Met a partner in crime and we were wed.
A life of pure love until our deathbed.
Course... my villainy she did not dilute.
If at all, she emboldened its pursuit!
"Hell is other people," someone once said.

But I can't agree. On mornings like this,
being condemned to hell is bearable.
We sip coffee, eat buttered scones. Share a kiss.
Maybe this makes for a bad parable,
but "life's" darn good down here in the abyss.
Heaven without her would not be comparable.

Everyone who ever loved me has left.
Laura just said something wasn't quite right.
Was Elizabeth turned off by my height?
Myra's breakup was subtle and deft,
(Though perhaps it had to do with that theft?)
No idea why Meg left, even in hindsight.
I just wish one of them had been forthright.
Why did they leave me of their love bereft?

I have to think that perhaps it's just me?
Each girl so different, yet all thought to balk.
It's the one thing on which they did agree.
But none of them has been willing to talk.
One more thing in common. Is that the key?
They all looked the same... when outlined in chalk.

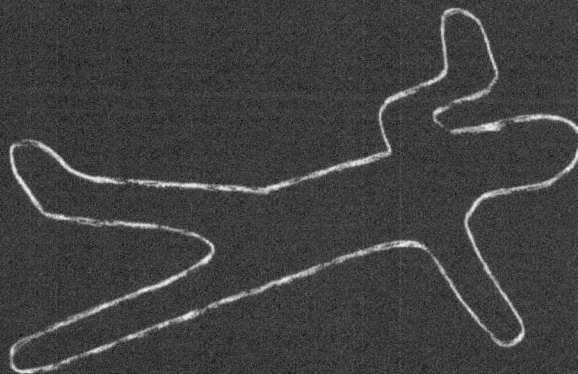

Divertente

As morning broke, they were already here.
A glint of cold metal high in the sky.
We were all somewhat scared, ain't gonna lie.
They came from deep space, have no idea where.
A loudspeaker appeared, started to blare,
"Take us to your leaders, make a reply!
"We have a treaty and gifts to supply!
"You've charmed us with your great blue and green sphere."

We gathered our leaders, Dems and Repubs,
in fancy silk suits, teeth white and hair combed.
"What?!?" said the spacemen, "You've sent us your scrubs!"
"These can't be your leaders! They're fools, morons, gnomes!"
We argued, but they'd been stung by the snubs.
They wouldn't believe us, and so flew on home.

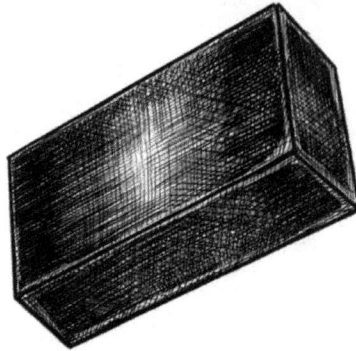

When I heard you'd taken ill, I wondered.
Happily, you took a turn for the worse.
"It doesn't look good at all," said the nurse.
Though for a while they held hope you'd be cured,
you fell into a coma, brow fevered.
I cheered as your ailment got more perverse,
and your eulogy I began to rehearse...
The end came when your heart at last ruptured.

I'm delighted you died when you got sick.
Eager for you to bid this world adieu.
I almost just smashed you with a lead brick.
(Even though I know murder is taboo.)
I'm glad this mortal coil you finally kicked.
T'was so lonely here in heaven without you.

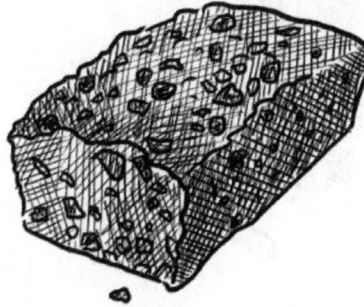

The last words you spoke as you boarded the train,
"I shall return to you on Christmas Day!"
Such a long time for you to be away...
Since you left, I've waited, half-crazed with pain.
Maybe something went bad inside my brain.
But I've slept every night in a red sleigh.
House filled with scents; holly, reindeers, and hay.
Why would that work? I could never explain.

But I kept the bunting up for seven years.
The tree withered and dead, for goodness sake.
It's time I gave up now, and faced my fears.
You'll never return, there's naught but heartbreak.
I at last broke down, and through Christmas tears,
opened your presents and ate your fruitcake.

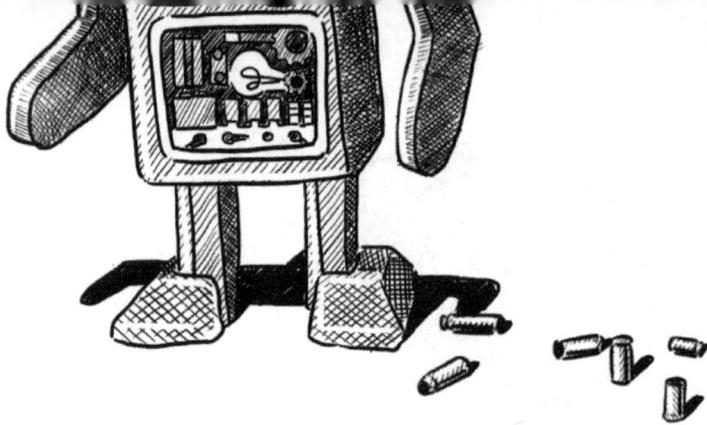

Robots smashed their way through our last line.
All defense gone, we were at their mercy.
Terms were offered, no choice but to agree.
Did the 'bots seek to murder all mankind?
Or maybe we'd end up toiling in mines?
We timidly listened to their decree,
but fright turned to relief, then to sheer glee,
as they enlightened us on their designs...

Turns out they were much more adept at rule,
than us petty humans ever could dream.
They were just tired of government by fool.
Robots made a better leadership team.
So we spent our days lounging by the pool.
They legislated, while we ate ice cream.

I read the origin of Spider-Man.
One small, mutant spider bite made him strong.
Toxic waste hit Daredevil's head like a gong.
He got superpowers, and lots of fans.
The Hulk could crush a tank like a tin can.
Zapped by gamma rays that did nothing wrong.
A mishap made Godzilla come along,
Nuclear waste was all part of his plan.

How come you hear all these crazy stories...
'bout people exposed who became fancier,
and went on to use their powers for glory?
I'm awful interested to hear your answer.
'cause that waste tank in the laboratory...
When I fell in, all I got was cancer.

I used to daydream about the end time.
A world devastated and mostly dead.
The human race hanging on by a thread.
Only me and a gorgeous girl in her prime.
And out of the wreckage, together we'd climb.
We'd learn how to forage, farm, and bake bread.
(and of course we'd fall in love and be wed..)
So sweet and so cute, even covered in grime.

I hope you can imagine my disdain,
when all that crawled from the rubble was you.
Since the collapse all you've done is complain.
You don't clean the house or cook me my stew.
Can't rebuild the world 'cause you're such a pain.
Hate being alone, but won't stay with a shrew.

The old women gathered around the table,
artfully set with flowers, cakes, and tea.
Where once were a dozen, now were only three.
"It's... nice having a life that is stable,
especially now that we're not quite as able."
She assumed that the others would both agree.
"I beg to differ, it's dull and beastly.
I'd kill for one last adventure, dear Mabel."

The three ladies gave each other sly glances,
and pulled cutlasses from under their gowns.
Pirate life had been full of romances,
so they loaded their flintlocks with fresh rounds.
On the high seas they'd again take their chances,
and find passion in foreign shanty-towns.

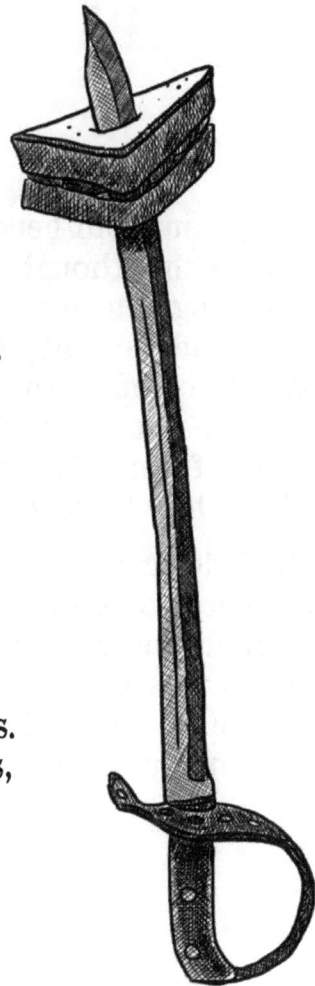

I'm contacting you from beyond the grave,
to let you know that though I'm dead and gone,
I'm still expecting you to carry on.
Don't be sad child, be a boy that's real brave.
Look up at that cloud in the sky and wave!
Maybe that's the one I'm sitting upon.
Hope you grow from ugly duckling to swan,
but more than that, I expect you'll behave.

So take a hint, let me be clear-cut.
No matter where you go or what you do,
whichever blinds you close or door you shut,
Granny's in heaven looking down on you;
in the park, the school, and toy store, but...
especially when you're alone in the loo.

We made camp on the Arctic Ocean's shore.
Huddled by the fire, waiting resupply,
Under the bleak and gray, darkening sky.
The crew was anxious, world-weary, and sore,
but still t'was an able and grizzled corps.
We told stories and jokes, both droll and dry,
and made fun of Tony the Cook's glass eye.
But soon came a madness we could not ignore.

Smith was the first to break, though not the last.
Attempted the journey solo with no guide.
He jumped into the sea from the fore-mast.
We looked on as he was lost in the tide.
Guess he couldn't wait for December to pass.
As he drowned, "I'm coming Santa!" he cried.

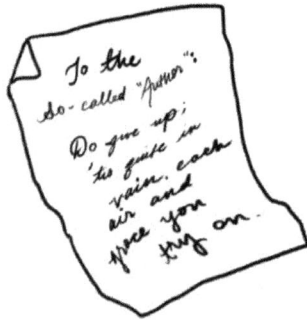

Publishing a sci-fi novel is hard!
I wrote one about a time-traveling witch.
But no agent wanted to hear my pitch.
At first, their rejections caught me off-guard,
and of my dignity left naught but a shard;
"The prose was pedantic, clichéd, and kitsch!"
"Terrible! Awful! Tossed it in a ditch!"
But, y'know? Those stings I'll just disregard.

I'm sure my work is destined for glory,
and it's certain their concerns I'll allay.
You see, my book is based on a true story...
and with every critique, I make headway.
Each iteration gets more laudatory,
and I'll go pitch it again yesterday.

They said Prue was too nice for witches' school.
"What's the point if you don't desire to curse?"
"Or if weak minds you don't care to coerce?"
All those labs spent with newts, herbs and toadstools,
seemed wasted time. Made her look like a fool.
Hester thought Prue should instead be a nurse.
Glinda told her to go major in verse.
But Prue felt magic taught skills that were cool.

For example, it was really handy,
to have built a voodoo doll of herself.
And give it backrubs and feed it candy.
Also, she learned to ensorcell an elf.
(a really tall one, dressed like a dandy).
Useful for retrieving things off her high shelf.

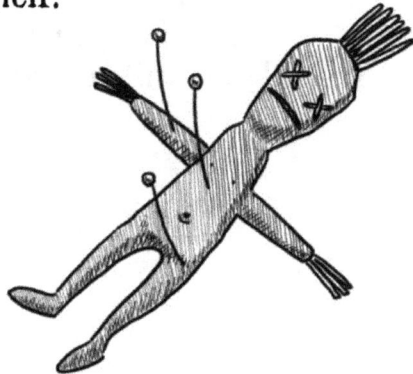

I remember the day you disappeared.
With nary a word you let go my hand,
and left without reason. Didn't seem planned.
Just floated away. I thought that was weird.
That you'd leave me was not something I'd feared.
So I kind of expected you to land.
But you flew up to... I guess somewhere grand?
Heaven perhaps? I wish I'd interfered.

But I just stood mute as you ascended.
Leaves rustling in trees was the only sound.
Have to think you're somewhere you intended.
I've given up hope someday you'll be found.
Wherever you've gone to, hope it's splendid.
I can still see your shadow on the ground.

I was gifted a magic looking-glass.
In that mirror was a horror perverse.
Held no mere image, but a whole universe.
A gate to an "opposite-land," in brass.
I quickly realized messages can pass,
when my reflection began to converse...
Said it's against the rules, had to be terse,
"But thanks so much for being a jackass!"

He was so glad I was his counterpart,
for each time I failed, that meant he'd succeed.
Because I'm so dumb, he gets to be smart.
Each time I screw up, he does a great deed.
I lost my true love, he won Martha's heart.
I smashed the mirror, in hope I'd be freed.

In time, everyone you have ever met,
will be dead. That concept is pretty plain.
And I don't think that I have to explain,
why every last child that they might beget,
also will die. No one left to forget;
who you were, how you lived, what you attained.
Then no one will ever think of you again.
You'll be totally gone, but don't get upset...

See, all those terrible mistakes you've made,
(Like the time you barfed on Meg at the prom)
won't matter at all once bodies are laid.
Know every bit of embarrassing drama,
from now won't be thought of in a decade.
So, pull up your pants and try to stay calm.

Epilogo

Every night as the sun was going down,
he scanned the seas for a light to guide him.
He was weary of long days carving scrim.
The hard, seafaring life just made him frown.
One night on a hill by a seaside town,
he spotted a fire burning, dying and dim.
He jumped off the deck. Started to swim.
Almost didn't reach shore before he did drown.

But don't fret, he made it. He was alright,
and ran soaking wet up the hill to her,
as she stood crying in a dress all of white.
Could it be him? Her eyes were a-blur.
He remembered her love. She held him tight.
"Tell me I'm home," he said in a whisper.

fine.

Circa l'autore

The author of this book has tried a number of methods to make people cry over the years — pulling their pigtails, putting spiders in their lunch, waterboarding, and telling them that he loves them when he knows in his heart it isn't true; but he's found that the most effective way by far is by writing disarmingly dumb stories about time machines and zombies and unrequited love.

One day, he somehow got it into his head to write more sonnets than Shakespeare, even though he had never written a poem before. So cut him some slack, he doesn't really know what he is doing.

Circa l'illustratore

Junnie Chup is an illustrator and the three-dimensional projection of an eleven-dimensional demonic entity, who currently resides in a small tear in the space-time continuum located just outside of Juneau, Alaska. She has illustrated several novels, as well as a children's book about dogs who like to dress up as food. The record remains stubbornly unclear regarding the question of whether she has ever written a poem before.

www.ingramcontent.com/pod-product-compliance
Lightning Source LLC
La Vergne TN
LVHW061331060426
835512LV00013B/2604